100 Reasons To Live

Dr. Divya Vachhani

Published independently by Dr. Divya Vachhani.

First Edition, 2026

For Siddharth, Saroja Di, and Bhargav Sir

This is for you;

Dr. Divya Vachhani

Contents

Dr. Divya Vachhani

Introduction

Do you ever feel like life is just too painful to go through? Like you're slowly running out of reasons to live?

Hi, I'm **Dr. Divya Vachhani**. I recently completed my MBBS. People think that being a doctor means your life is all figured out, that you are tough and capable, and that you know how to help people. However, I have spent most of my life not knowing how to help myself.

There were days when surviving felt difficult, days when waking up felt like a burden rather than a blessing. I wasn't looking for happiness anymore, I was simply looking for one reason to stay.

Just one.

When I couldn't find a big reason, I began searching for small ones: the warmth of the morning sun, a familiar song, the smell of coffee, a stranger's kindness, the quiet comfort of knowing that tomorrow hadn't happened yet, tiny, ordinary moments that reminded me that life wasn't asking me to have all the answers, it was only asking me to stay a little longer.

Slowly, those small reasons became enough to carry me through another day.

And somewhere along this journey, a book was born.

100 Reasons to Live isn't a cure for pain. It isn't a promise that life will suddenly become beautiful. Some days will still hurt. Some days will still feel unbearably heavy. But I've learned that even on the darkest days, hope doesn't always arrive as a beautiful sunrise. Sometimes, it comes as the faintest light just enough to help you take one more step.

This book is a collection of those small lights.

I wrote it for the version of myself who believed there was nothing left to hold on to, and for anyone who has ever felt the same.

If you're reading this with a heavy heart, I hope these pages remind you that your story doesn't have to end where your pain begins.

I hope that somewhere within these pages, you find a reason to stay.

And then another. And another. Until one day, you realize you have a hundred.

— Dr. Divya Vachhani

Prologue

This book is written by someone who has experienced bereavement and loss through suicide. These pages are shaped by grief, love, and the words that were never spoken or never heard. After experiencing the devastating impact of suicide, the author has taken it upon herself to ensure that others feel seen, heard, and supported.

Some of the things she longed to hear were words of comfort, but no one said them. So, she has placed those unheard words within these pages for anyone who may need them. Through words of comfort, stories of what happened, what could have happened, and the things she wishes she could still do or say, she hopes to offer a little light to those walking through darkness.

This book is not a substitute for psychotherapy, crisis support, or medical care. Rather, it is intended to sit alongside them as a quiet companion, offering comfort, understanding, and gentle reminders that hope still exists, even on the hardest and darkest days.

Above all, this book is a gentle reminder that no one should have to earn help, and no one should ever feel like a burden.

Think of this book as your sunflower. Even in darkness, two sunflowers can stand beside one another, borrowing hope until they find the light again.

If this book is your sunflower, then I am honoured to be the sunflower to its author, Dr. Divya Vachhani. Through every season of grief, hope, and healing, I have had the privilege of witnessing the compassion that inspired these pages. This book is a reflection of the kindness, strength, and love she continues to share with others.

My name is Chaitanyaa Ashish Sachde. I am a psychology graduate with a background in cognitive neuroscience, a mental health advocate, and an author. Through my work in psychology, neurorehabilitation, and mental health awareness, I am committed to making psychological support more accessible and reducing the stigma surrounding mental illness. Having witnessed the profound impact of suicide and psychological pain, I believe that compassion, hope, and human connection can be powerful companions on the journey towards healing.

My relationship with Divya goes far beyond friendship. She is my sister. We may not be related by blood, but we are connected by love, trust, and unwavering support. I have witnessed the untold story behind every page you are about to read the grief that shaped it, the strength it demanded, and the hope that emerged from it. It is a privilege and an honour to write this prologue and to stand beside Divya as she courageously shares her heart with the world.

– Chaitanyaa Ashish Sachde

"Sometimes, small reasons are enough to help us make it through one more day."

Dr. Divya Vachhani

Because, You're Reading This Book

You don't have to believe me yet.

If you've picked up this book because you're searching for a reason to stay, I'm glad you're here.

I don't know your story. I don't know what you've lost, what you're carrying, or what brought you to these pages.

But I know what it feels like when your mind convinces you that there is nothing left worth holding on to.

I know what it feels like to wake up already tired. To smile while quietly falling apart. To wonder if everyone else received a handbook on how to live that you somehow missed.

This book isn't asking you to suddenly love life. It isn't asking you to become positive. It isn't asking you to be grateful for your suffering.

It is only asking you to stay with me for a little while. Maybe one page. Maybe one reason.

Maybe today, that's enough.

Because, My Therapy Homework Got Out Of Hand

My therapist, in a moment of questionable confidence, called me a *"hardworking client"*. I don't know if she meant it as a compliment or if she was politely saying, *"You are going to make me earn my therapist salary."*

Because here I am, turning my reasons to live into a book.

A normal person gets therapy homework and writes a few bullet points. I apparently thought: *"What if I write 100 reasons, edit them, organise them into chapters, and publish them?"*

Overachiever? Maybe. Dramatic? Absolutely. But honestly, I love that my therapist saw something in me that I sometimes forget. She saw someone who was still trying, someone who showed up, someone who did the homework, even if the homework accidentally became a whole book.

I used to think healing meant having everything figured out. Turns out, sometimes healing looks like sitting with your therapist, being handed homework, and thinking: *"Well… I guess I have to do this now."*

So here I am, doing my homework, just slightly more publicly than intended.

Because, 'I Want To' Want to Get Better

For the longest time, people asked me if I wanted to get better. I always said yes. But somewhere deep inside, I wasn't so sure.

Not because I wanted to stay in pain, but because, I had become so tired of carrying it that even healing felt exhausting. I wasn't dreaming of a better life anymore. I was just trying to survive this one.

That scared me. Because, I realised I didn't just lose the desire to get better. I lost the desire to *want* to get better.

Maybe that's what pain does. It convinces you that there's nothing waiting for you on the other side.

But I don't want to believe that forever.

I want to know what it feels like to wake up one day and genuinely want to fight for myself. To choose life not because I have to, but because I want to.

I haven't met that version of me yet. And maybe… That's reason enough to stay. Because she deserves a chance to exist.

Because, I Want People To Know They Aren't Alone

I know what it feels like to believe that no one could possibly understand what is happening inside your mind.

To smile while you're struggling. To answer, "I'm fine," because explaining the truth feels impossible. To wonder if anyone else has ever felt this lost, this exhausted, this overwhelmed.

I don't want anyone to carry that kind of loneliness by themselves.

If my story, my words, or simply my presence can help even one person think, *"Me too. I thought I was the only one,"* then they will have served a purpose greater than I could have imagined.

I want people to know that there is no shame in asking for help. That surviving doesn't make you weak. That healing is rarely neat, and that struggling doesn't make you a burden.

Sometimes we don't need someone to solve our pain. We just need someone to sit beside us and remind us that we're not the only ones walking through it.

I want to be that reminder.

Because no one should have to feel like they are fighting their hardest battles in complete silence.

I want to live long enough to tell people, with complete sincerity, *"You're not alone. I'm here. And there is still hope."*

Because, Post-it Notes On My Wall

A few years ago, I started writing one Post-it note for every day I chose to stay.

I don't know why that idea came to me after nearly a decade of struggling with my health. Maybe I had finally reached a point where I needed something I could see. Something that reminded me that even on the days that felt impossible, I was still here.

So every day I chose to stay alive, I wrote a note.

Sometimes it was a quote. Sometimes it was a thought I didn't want to forget. Sometimes it was just enough to get me through that day.

Then I stuck it on my wall.

At first, there were only a handful. Then a few more. Before I knew it, the wall had begun to fill.

When I look at it now, I don't see colourful pieces of paper. I see thousands of quiet decisions, days I thought I wouldn't survive, but somehow did, days where staying felt like the hardest thing I'd ever done, days that asked everything of me, and still ended with one more Post-it on the wall.

No single note is extraordinary. But together, they tell the story of a person who kept choosing tomorrow, even when she couldn't see what tomorrow would bring.

That wall reminds me of something I often forget: I've done this before. I've survived difficult days before.

And maybe, just maybe… I can do it again tomorrow

.

Because, I Want To Meet The Version Of Me That Lives In Peace

I don't think I've ever wanted a grand life.

People dream of becoming rich, famous, or wildly successful. Somewhere along the way, I realised that wasn't what I wanted at all.

I just want peace.

The kind of peace where my heart doesn't race for no reason. Where every notification doesn't make me anxious. Where a loud sound doesn't make my body jump before my mind has a chance to understand that I'm safe.

I want to know what it feels like to live without constantly bracing for something bad to happen.

I wonder what it's like to have a nervous system that isn't exhausted from trying to protect you all the time. To go to bed without replaying the day over and over again. To wake up without feeling like you've already run a marathon before your feet have even touched the floor.

I wonder what it feels like when your mind becomes a place you enjoy spending time in.

I don't know that version of myself yet. The version whose shoulders aren't always tense. The version who doesn't overthink every conversation. The version who isn't haunted by memories that still feel like they're happening all over again. The version who can sit in silence without being afraid of her own thoughts.

But I like to believe she exists. Maybe she's waiting for me somewhere in the future. Maybe she's sitting on a balcony with a cup of tea, watching the rain without feeling overwhelmed by it. Maybe she laughs more easily. Maybe she sleeps through the night. Maybe she doesn't have to fight herself just to make it through the day.

I'd like to meet her. I'd like to know what it feels like to wake up one morning and realise that surviving is no longer my full-time job.

That I'm finally living. I don't need a perfect life. I don't even need a happy life. I just want a gentle one. One where my mind finally learns that it doesn't have to be at war with itself anymore.

Because, somewhere ahead of me is a version of myself I've never had the chance to become. I'd like to give her that chance.

Because, Rain

I've always imagined myself sitting on a pavement in the pouring rain whenever life becomes too much. I don't know why.

Maybe it's because the sky feels like it's crying with me, and for a little while, I don't have to cry alone. Maybe it's because every raindrop reminds me that I can still feel something outside of the ache in my chest. Or maybe it's because rain asks nothing of me. It doesn't tell me to smile, to be grateful, or to look on the bright side. It simply falls.

When my thoughts become too loud, I imagine the rain washing over them. I imagine sitting there, letting every drop land on my skin until I can finally hear something other than the noise in my own head. It's a great way to ground yourself.

My body always seems to carry a fever these days. The rain cools me down. It reminds me that I have a body, that I'm breathing, that I'm here.

So when there isn't any rain, I imagine it. I imagine dancing in it. I imagine sitting quietly on the pavement, letting the world disappear into the sound of falling water. I imagine that beautiful smell that reminds me of love and peace.

And when it finally does rain, maybe I'll find the courage to step outside instead of watching it through my window. Maybe I'll let it soak my clothes. Maybe I'll let it remind me that storms don't only exist to destroy.

Sometimes, they come to soften the earth. Sometimes, they come to soften us.

And sometimes, they give us one more reason to stay.

Because, That One Person

I have a friend. My sister from another mother.

She checks in on me every single day. Sometimes, every few hours. She'll ask if I've eaten, if I've taken my medications, if I managed to sleep the night before. If I tell her I'm tired, she'll ask why. If I disappear for a while, she'll notice. She always notices.

For the longest time, I never understood why someone would care that much.

I used to think I was difficult to love. That I was too much, too emotional, too broken. But somehow, she never made me feel like I was a burden. She never made checking in feel like an obligation. She simply... showed up. Again and again.

There have been days when I haven't had the energy to reply. Days when I wanted to switch my phone off and disappear from the world for a while. But then I'd see her name on my screen.

"Have you eaten?"

"Did you take your meds?"

"Just checking in."

Three ordinary messages.

Three ordinary questions.

And yet, they have pulled me back more times than she'll ever know.

It's strange how something so small can make you feel so deeply loved. To know that somewhere, someone is wondering whether you've had lunch. Whether you're sleeping enough. Whether you've made it home safely.

In a world that moves so quickly, being remembered feels like a kind of love.

There were days when I couldn't find a reason to stay for myself. My own hope had become too quiet to hear. On those days, I stayed because someone else believed I should.

I borrowed her hope until I could find my own.

And maybe that's okay.

Maybe healing doesn't always begin with loving yourself. Maybe, sometimes, it begins with letting someone love you until you remember that you're worth loving too.

If you're lucky enough to have that one person, the one who checks in, who notices, who refuses to let you disappear quietly… hold them close.

They may never know it. But sometimes… One person is enough.

One person can become a reason to stay.

Because, I Haven't Found The Love Of My Life Yet

Sometimes I wonder if we've already crossed paths without knowing it. Maybe we've stood in the same coffee shop, walked on the same street, or waited at the same airport gate. Maybe we've been living completely different lives, unaware that one day our stories might become the same story.

Or maybe we've never been anywhere near each other.

I don't know. But I like knowing that I don't know. It is strangely comforting about the fact that my greatest love story might still be waiting for me.

I haven't fallen in love with someone who feels like home yet. I haven't experienced the kind of love where silence isn't awkward, where I can cry without apologising, where I don't have to pretend I'm okay just to make someone else comfortable. I haven't met the person who sees every complicated, messy part of me and decides to stay anyway.

I wonder what it will feel like to finally be the one. To have someone look at me not because they have to, but because they want to. To have someone learn all the little things about me. That I need the fan on even when it's raining. That I always stop to watch sunsets. That rain calms me down. That I overthink everything. That I take forever to decide what to eat. That I laugh too loudly when I'm genuinely happy.

I wonder what it will feel like when someone knows all of those things… and loves me even more because of them.

I think about the life I haven't lived yet. The first time someone reaches for my hand without thinking. The first "I'm so glad I found you." The first home we build together. The first ordinary Tuesday that somehow feels extraordinary because we're living it together.

I think about growing old with someone. About grey hair and wrinkles and cups of tea on quiet mornings. About sitting beside each other in comfortable silence, knowing that after everything life threw at us, we still chose each other.

Maybe I'm a hopeless romantic. Or maybe I'm just hopeful. Because if I leave too soon, I'll never know what his voice sounds like when he says my name. I'll never know what it feels like to wear the dress I've imagined since I was a little girl. I'll never know what it's like to promise someone forever and actually get to live it. I'll never know what it feels like to come home to the person who makes the world feel a little less heavy.

Maybe he exists. Maybe he doesn't. But if he does… I'd like to stay long enough to find him.

And maybe, somewhere out there, he's hoping he'll find me too.

Because, The Sun Always Comes Back

I've survived nights that felt like they would never end. The kind where sleep doesn't come easily, and neither do hopeful thoughts.

Then morning arrives. I don't always notice it at first. But eventually, the sunlight reaches me.

It settles softly on my skin, warming my face as if it's saying, *"You made it through another night."*

I don't take those mornings for granted anymore. I've learned that the sun has never failed to return. Even when I thought it might.

Maybe that's why I keep believing that hope can return too.

Because, Children Still Laugh

Sometimes, I'll be walking past a park when I hear it before I see it.

Laughter.

The kind that is loud, uninhibited, and completely free.

I find myself slowing down, almost without realizing it. I watch children chase each other across the grass, trip over their own feet, get back up, and burst into laughter as though nothing in the world could possibly weigh them down.

Their innocence is beautiful. They aren't worrying about tomorrow. They aren't replaying conversations from last week. They aren't wondering whether they're good enough, productive enough, or lovable enough.

They're just… living.

And sometimes I catch myself thinking, '*Once, I was like that too*'. Once, I laughed without wondering what came next. Once, my biggest worry was whether I could stay at the park for five more minutes. Once, I didn't know what anxiety felt like. I didn't know what it meant to carry grief, heartbreak, burnout, or the invisible weight that adulthood quietly places on our shoulders.

Life changed. I changed.

But when I watch children laugh, I like to believe that the part of me that knew joy so effortlessly isn't gone forever.

Maybe she's just been buried beneath years of trying to survive. Maybe she's still there, waiting patiently for me.

If a one-year-old can find endless joy in chasing bubbles, splashing through puddles, or watching a butterfly flutter by, maybe life doesn't always have to be as complicated as I've made it.

Maybe joy isn't something we lose. Maybe it's something we slowly learn to return to.

I don't expect to become that carefree child again. Life has taught me too much for that. But I hope that one day, I'll laugh from my stomach again. I hope that one day, I'll find wonder in ordinary things. I hope that one day, I'll stop rushing through life long enough to notice the butterflies too.

And until then… I'll keep smiling at the children in the park. Because, every time they laugh, they remind me that joy exists.

And if it exists for them today, maybe, one day, it can exist for me again.

Because, I Don't Know If There's Pizza Or Ice Cream After We Die

I don't know what happens after we die. Maybe there's another life. Maybe there's nothing at all. Maybe there's a heaven with endless sunsets and people we've missed for years.

I honestly don't know.

But here's what I *do* know. I've never seen any evidence that there's pizza. Or ice cream. And until someone comes back to confirm otherwise, I think I'd rather stay here.

Because, there are still pizzas I haven't tried. Ice cream flavours I haven't tasted. Late-night dessert runs with people I love still waiting for me.

The kind where you laugh so hard that your stomach hurts more than it would have if you'd skipped dessert.

Maybe it sounds silly. Maybe it is. But life isn't only made of extraordinary moments. Sometimes it's melted chocolate on your fingers. Sometimes it's stealing the last slice of pizza. Sometimes it's deciding that calories can wait until tomorrow.

I think we spend so much time searching for life's biggest purpose that we forget how much joy lives in the smallest things.

So yes… One of my reasons to stay is pizza. And ice cream.

Because, if this is the only place I get to enjoy them, I think I'll have another slice.

Just to be safe.

Because, I'm Not Done Writing This Book

There were days when I genuinely didn't think I would live long enough to write these words. Days when the future felt so distant that even tomorrow seemed impossible.

And yet, here I am, one page at a time, one sentence at a time, slowly turning pain into something that might one day become hope for someone else.

Maybe this book found me before I was ready for it. Maybe I needed to live through everything I did so I could write the words I once desperately needed to read.

Every chapter I finish feels like quiet proof that I survived another day. Every reason I write becomes another reason I choose to stay. I don't know who you are, or where you'll be when you read this, but maybe one day you'll pick up this book on a day when life feels unbearably heavy, and maybe one sentence will make you pause long enough to stay.

If that happens, then every tear that went into these pages will have been worth it.

I owe it to the younger version of me, the one who never thought she'd have a story worth telling. I owe it to the future version of me, who deserves to see this book resting on a shelf, held in someone's hands, quietly reminding them that they are not alone.

And until I write the very last word, until I hold this finished book and know that a piece of my heart now exists in the world, I don't think I'm done living either.

Neither am I done writing. There will be more books, I promise.

Because, I Promised Someone I Would Live

There are people I wish I could have had just one more conversation with.

People whose laughter I can still hear if I close my eyes. People whose absence still catches me off guard, even after all this time.

When they died by suicide, they took pieces of my heart with them.

For a long time, I kept asking questions that had no answers. I replayed conversations. I wondered if there was something I could have said, something I should have noticed, something that could have changed the ending. Grief has a cruel way of making you believe you could have rewritten someone else's story.

One day, I realised I couldn't. But I could choose what I did with mine. So I made them a promise.

I promised that I would live.

Not because living suddenly became easy, but because they never got the chance to keep writing their stories. They never got to grow older, fall in love, watch another sunrise, or become the people they were still becoming.

I did.

Some days, when life feels unbearably heavy, I think of them. I wonder what they would have given for one more ordinary day. One more cup of coffee. One more rainy afternoon. One more chance to tell someone they loved them.

So on the days when I can't live for myself, I remember my promise.

I choose to notice the sunsets. I choose to stand in the rain. I choose to keep writing. I choose to stay.

Because, if I can carry a little more life into this world in their memory, then a part of them continues to exist through the way I choose to live.

And I think... That is a promise worth keeping.

Because, They Were Wrong

There are some sentences you will never forget.

During a viva in medical school, a professor looked at me and told me to jump off the sixth floor of my college.

I don't know if they remember saying it. I do.

It's strange how the mind holds on to moments like that. You can forget what you had for breakfast yesterday, but somehow, years later, you can still remember the exact words that broke your spirit.

For a long time, those words followed me. On my darkest days, they echoed louder than my own voice. They made me question whether I really was as worthless as someone had made me feel.

But then I thought, if I let those words become the end of my story, then I would be giving someone else the power to write a life that was never theirs to write.

They don't get that. They don't get to decide whether I deserve to be here. They don't get to decide whether my life is worth living.

I do. So I stayed.

I finished medical school.

I became a doctor.

I’m still here.

I choose to believe that my story deserves a far more beautiful ending than the one they imagined for me.

Because, Someone Will Need Your Story

For the longest time, I thought all I was doing was surviving.

Every other day, I found myself sitting in another doctor's waiting room. Most days, I functioned with a pain score of five and a distress level of seven out of a ten before the day had even begun. It became so normal that I stopped thinking of it as courage. I was just trying to get through another day.

I never thought anyone was watching.

One day, during medical school, one of my classmates stood up and said something I'll never forget.

"If she can do it, with the amount of suffering she lives with, then surely we can too. Looking at her gives me the courage to get through medical training."

I don't think they realised what those words did to me. Because all I could see was someone who was barely holding herself together. I never realised that someone else was looking at the exact same person and seeing resilience.

That day changed something in me. It made me realise that maybe our stories aren't meant to be hidden because they're messy. Maybe they're meant to be told.

You never really know who's watching you quietly. You never know who sees your strength before you do. You never know who finds hope simply because you chose to show up, even when showing up felt impossible.

Maybe one day, someone will read your story on a day when they feel like giving up. Maybe they'll see parts of themselves in your words. Maybe they'll think, *"If they made it through that, maybe I can make it through this."*

You may never know whose life you touch. You may never know whose courage begins with your story.

But I'd like to stay long enough to tell mine. Because maybe, just maybe... Someone out there is waiting to read it.

Because, A Patient Asked Me If I Always Smile

A patient once looked at me and asked, *"Doctor, do you always smile?"*

I smiled a little wider. Not because life had been kind to me that day. But because, for those few minutes, my pain wasn't the most important thing in the room. Theirs was.

Most people don't see what happens before I walk into the hospital. They don't see the pain I wake up with, the appointments, the medications, or the days when simply getting out of bed feels like an achievement. By the time I put on my white coat, I've often already fought battles no one knows about.

And yet, when I step into a patient's room, something changes. I want them to feel seen. I want them to feel heard. I want them to feel like, for those few moments, they are the only person who matters.

Because that's what I would want if I were lying in that bed. So yes, I smile. Not because I'm pretending everything is okay. But because sometimes a smile is the first medicine we can offer another human being.

It's the quiet reassurance that says, *"I'm here with you."*

The beautiful thing is, I often walk in thinking I'm the one who has come to help. But somehow, my patients help me too. Their stories remind me how deeply human we all are. Their resilience humbles me. Their trust is a privilege I'll never stop being grateful for.

I realised something after that patient asked me if I always smiled. Maybe I do smile a little more than I need to. Not because I don't hurt. But because I love bringing smiles to faces that have forgotten how to smile.

And somehow... Every time I make someone else's day a little lighter, mine becomes a little lighter too.

That, too, is a reason to stay.

Because, You May Never Know Who You Saved

We often think changing someone's life has to look extraordinary. A dramatic rescue. The perfect words. A heroic act.

But most of the time, it doesn't. Sometimes it's answering a phone call. Sometimes it's sitting beside someone in silence. Sometimes it's staying after everyone else has left. Sometimes it's simply being kind on a day someone was convinced the world had forgotten them.

The truth is, you'll probably never know the impact you've had on other people's lives. Maybe you helped someone through the darkest week of their life without even realizing it. Maybe you listened when everyone else was too busy. Maybe you believed in someone before they believed in themselves. Maybe your kindness became the reason they made it through another day.

We rarely get to see the full story. We don't always find out that the conversation we barely remember became something another person never forgot.

I like to believe that our lives leave fingerprints on the people we meet. Small ones. Quiet ones. The kind that changes someone's life without either of you noticing at the time.

And maybe that's true for the future, too. Maybe there are people you haven't met yet who will need your kindness. A patient who will need your reassurance. A friend who will need your listening ear. A stranger who will one day cross paths with you at exactly the right moment.

You don't have to change the whole world. Sometimes, changing one person's world is enough.

And maybe... Without even knowing it, you already have.

And maybe there are still lives waiting to be touched simply because you chose to stay.

Because, I'll Never Get to Eat Pani Puri With My Family Again

It's funny how the smallest moments become the ones we miss the most.

Just an evening spent standing around a pani puri stall with my family, arguing over who gets the last one, laughing at whoever asked for "extra spicy" and instantly regretting it.

Those moments never feel extraordinary while they're happening. They're just… life. Until one day, you realise they won't last forever.

One day, there will be a last family dinner. A last festival celebrated together. A last cup of chai. A last plate of pani puri shared between people you love.

That thought breaks my heart. Not because I think that day is near, but because it reminds me how precious today really is.

I'd like to have as many of those evenings as I possibly can. I'd like to stand around that stall a few hundred more times. To laugh until my stomach hurts. To complain that it's too spicy, only to ask for another one anyway. To look around and realise that everyone I love is still standing beside me.

One day, memories will be all I have. But today… Today, I still have the chance to make new ones.

And I think that's reason enough to stay.

Because, I Know What It Leaves Behind

I've lost people I loved to suicide. More than once.

There aren't enough words to describe what that kind of grief feels like. It isn't just sadness. It's shock, disbelief, guilt, anger, longing, and a thousand unanswered questions that never seem to leave you.

You keep wondering if there was something you missed. Something you should have said. Something you could have done. You replay conversations in your head until you know them by heart, hoping that somewhere in them you'll find a different ending.

You don't. The hardest part isn't just losing the person. It's learning to live with the space they leave behind.

I've seen what suicide does to the people who stay. I've seen birthdays that suddenly feel incomplete. Chairs that remain empty. Phones that no longer ring. Families that are never quite the same again.

I know what it feels like to carry that kind of loss. And because I know, I also know something else. If I were to leave, the people who love me would carry that same weight. They would ask the same impossible questions. They would replay the same memories. They would wonder if there was something they could have done differently.

I don't want that for them. Not because I think my life exists only for the people I love, but because I know how deeply love and grief are intertwined.

The people who love us don't just lose us. They carry us for the rest of their lives.

So on the days when staying feels impossibly hard, I think of the people who would have to learn to live with my absence. I think of the love we've shared.

And I choose, as best as I can, to stay with them a little longer. Because I've lived through the heartbreak of losing someone. And if I can spare the people I love from carrying that same heartbreak, then today…

That is reason enough to live.

Because, Maybe I'm Not Broken To Be Fixed

For the longest time, I believed I was a project: something to fix, something to repair. Every difficult emotion, every bad day, every panic attack, every scar felt like another piece of evidence that there was something fundamentally wrong with me.

So I spent years trying to become someone else. Someone who didn't hurt this much. Someone who didn't overthink. Someone who wasn't so tired all the time.

Then one day, my therapist looked at me and said something I'll never forget.

"You don't need to fix yourself, because you're not broken."

I didn't know what to say. I had spent so long believing that I was broken that I had never stopped to question whether it was even true. Maybe I wasn't broken. Maybe I was hurting. Maybe there is a difference.

That one sentence didn't erase my pain. It didn't magically make life easier. But it gave me something I hadn't had in a very long time. It gave me permission to stop treating myself like a problem.

Maybe healing isn't about becoming a different person. Maybe it's about learning to be gentler with the person you've been all along.

I’d like to stay long enough to believe that.

Maybe one day… I will.

Because, There Are Places That Have Yet to Learn My Name

Sometimes I forget how big the world really is.

I get so caught up in hospital appointments, deadlines, difficult days, and the familiar streets I walk every week that my world begins to feel very small.

Then I remember there are cities I've never wandered through. Mountains I've never stood beneath. Beaches I've never watched the sunrise from. Cafés where no one knows my name yet. There are places that have yet to learn my footsteps. Places that have yet to hear my laughter. Places that have yet to learn my name.

I wonder what kind of person I'll be when I meet them. Maybe I'll be a little lighter. Maybe I'll finally breathe deeply without even realizing it.

Maybe I'll sit alone in a little café halfway across the world, watching strangers live their ordinary lives, and suddenly feel grateful that I stayed long enough to witness mine.

The beautiful thing about travel isn't just discovering new places. It's discovering new versions of yourself. The version of you who says yes to adventure. The version who gets lost and laughs instead of panicking. The version who watches a sunset from a place she once only saw in photographs and quietly thinks,

"I'm really here."

I don't know where life will take me. But I know there are roads I haven't walked, skies I haven't looked up at, and places that are still waiting for me.

I'd like to meet them. And maybe… I'd like them to learn my name.

Because, I Want to Learn to Paint Again

There was a time when painting came naturally to me. I could sit for hours with a blank canvas and a handful of colours, and somehow, the world felt a little quieter. I painted because it made me happy. I painted because I could create something beautiful, even when life wasn't.

Then depression arrived. Slowly, quietly, it took things from me that I didn't even notice at first. One of those things was painting. It's been almost a decade now.

Every now and then, I'll walk past an art store or see someone mixing colours on a canvas, and something inside me aches. Not because I can't paint anymore, but because I remember the girl who once could. I miss her.

I miss the version of me who reached for a paintbrush without overthinking it. The one who found joy in creating instead of merely surviving.

I'd like to meet her again. Maybe one day, I'll buy a fresh canvas. Maybe my hands will feel clumsy at first. Maybe I'll forget how to mix the colours I used to know by heart.

That's okay. I'll learn. Brushstroke by brushstroke. I want to paint flowers again. Beautiful faces. Skies filled with stars.

Little pieces of beauty that remind me that not everything depression took has to stay lost forever. Maybe healing isn't getting back the exact person I used to be. Maybe it's picking up the paintbrush anyway. And seeing who I become.

I'd like to stay long enough to find out.

Because, I Don't Have to Earn My Place Here

For a long time, I thought I had to earn my right to exist. I thought I had to achieve more. Work harder. Be kinder. Be more successful. Be less emotional. Less complicated. Less… me. As though my existence had to be justified. As though I had to prove that I deserved the space I occupied in this world.

But when I really think about it, no one asks a newborn baby to earn their place here. No one asks a flower why it bloomed. No one asks the rain to explain why it falls. They simply exist. Maybe I'm allowed to exist that way too. Not because I've achieved enough. Not because I've suffered enough. Not because I've spent my whole life trying to be useful to everyone around me. Simply because I'm here.

I didn't choose to be born. One day, I opened my eyes to this world, and somehow, I became part of it.

There was a day when one of my teachers asked the whole class, "what's that one right that you get as soon as you're born?" And I instantly said, "The right to Live." The teacher asked the whole class to clap for me. I was barely 15 years old then. I look back at that moment sometimes.

Maybe I don't have to spend the rest of my life apologising for taking up space. Maybe I don't have to justify every breath I take. Maybe existing is enough.

And if life has already made room for me, perhaps I can stop questioning whether I belong here.

Perhaps I can trust that my place doesn't have to be earned. It has already been given.

Because, Feelings Are Visitors

My therapist once said something to me that completely changed the way I looked at my emotions.

"Feelings are visitors."

I remember sitting there, quietly thinking, *That can't be true.* Because if you've lived with depression or anxiety for long enough, they don't feel like visitors. They feel like they've signed a long-term lease. They settle into your life so comfortably that you begin to believe they'll always be there. I certainly did.

There were days I was convinced I'd never laugh the same way again. Never feel excited about anything again. Never wake up and think, *Today might be okay.*

But then something strange would happen. I'd have a good afternoon. I'd find myself smiling at a child in the supermarket. I'd laugh at something my friend said. I'd enjoy the rain. And for a few moments, I'd realise that the sadness had quietly stepped out of the room.

It came back, of course. But so did those little moments. That's when I understood what she meant. Feelings don't stay still. Not even the painful ones.

They ebb and flow like the tide. Some stay longer than we'd like. Some visit so often that they start to feel familiar. But none of them are the whole story.

Now, when I have a particularly difficult day, I try not to tell myself, *This is my life.*

I tell myself, *This is how today feels.*

Somehow, that feels lighter. It reminds me that today doesn't get to speak for tomorrow. That this moment doesn't get to decide the rest of my life.

Maybe joy is already on its way, quietly making its journey back to me. Maybe peace is too. I just haven't opened the door to them yet.

So today, I'll let this feeling visit. I'll make it a cup of tea if I have to. But I won't let it convince me that it owns the house. Because I know, deep down, that visitors eventually leave.

And I'd like to stay long enough to welcome the next one.

Because, My Therapist Told Me My Life Matters

There was a day when my therapist looked at me and quietly said, *"Your life matters to me."*

I don't think she'll ever know what those words did to me. When you've spent so long wondering whether the world would notice if you disappeared, hearing someone say your life matters feels almost unbelievable.

I didn't know how badly I needed to hear it until I did.

I still carry those words with me. On the days when I can't believe my life matters to me, I borrow her belief instead.

Just for a little while. Until I can believe it too.

Because, My Post-it Notes Are Shaped Like Tiny T-Shirts

I own Post-it notes shaped like little T-shirts. I don't know why. I don't know who looked at a sticky note and thought, *You know what this needs? Sleeves.*

But every time I use one, I smile. Sometimes I even laugh not because it's the funniest thing in the world, but because it's so wonderfully unnecessary.

On difficult days, I've realised I don't always need something life-changing to make me feel a little better. Sometimes I just need something delightfully absurd.

A tiny T-shirt-shaped sticky note. A reminder that the world is full of people who spend their time creating things that don't have to exist, but do anyway.

And somehow… That makes me smile. It reminds me that joy doesn't always arrive in grand moments.

Sometimes it arrives as a sticky note wearing a tiny imaginary T-shirt.

Because, "Mann Ka Ho Toh Accha, Na Ho Toh Aur Bhi Accha"

If things happen the way you want, that's good. If they don't, perhaps something even better is waiting.

I'll admit, there were many days I rolled my eyes at those words. Because when your heart is breaking, when you've lost something you desperately wanted, the last thing you want to hear is that it's "for the best."

It doesn't feel like it. It just hurts. But life has a strange way of teaching us things only in hindsight.

Some of the things I begged for would have broken me if I'd received them. Some of the doors that closed led me to people I would never have met otherwise. Some endings made room for beginnings I couldn't have imagined. I still don't understand every disappointment. I still have questions that may never have answers.

But somewhere along the way, I've learned to loosen my grip a little. To believe that not everything I lose is a punishment. Sometimes, it's life gently making space for something I haven't seen yet. That thought comforts me.

Not because it promises that everything will work out perfectly, but because it reminds me that my story isn't finished. There are still people I haven't met. Places I haven't seen. Dreams I haven't dreamed yet. Maybe they're already making their way towards me. Maybe all I have to do is stay long enough for them to arrive.

And until they do… I'll keep a little corner of my heart open.

Just in case life has something even more beautiful planned than anything I could have imagined for myself.

Because, I've Already Survived So Much

Sometimes I catch myself thinking, *Surely life has to run out of plot twists eventually.*

I've been through more than I ever thought I could survive. The kind of years that change you. The kind that leaves scars no one else can see.

There were moments I was certain would break me. Somehow, they didn't. I'm still here.

I won't pretend nothing else can go wrong. Life doesn't make those kinds of promises. But after everything I've already lived through, I've stopped underestimating myself.

I've learned that I'm stronger than I ever wanted to have to be. If I've survived every day that I once believed would destroy me, maybe I can survive this one too.

And who knows? Maybe the next surprise won't be another storm.

Maybe it'll be peaceful.

Because, Not Everyone Knows My Road

I have spent a lot of time listening to people tell me what I should do. And sometimes, I forget to ask myself a simple question:

"Have they ever walked where I am walking?"

Because it is easy to give directions from the sidelines. The truth is, not everyone will understand my choices. Not everyone will understand my pace. Not everyone will understand why some things that look small to them feel enormous to me.

And that's okay. They are seeing a small part of my story. I am the one who has lived every chapter. I can listen to advice. I can learn from others.

But I don't have to hand over the steering wheel of my life to someone who has never sat in my seat. This is my road, my journey.

And I am allowed to find my own way. Because what is life without its challenges?

Because, Sunflowers Are Inspiring

I once read that when the sun disappears and darkness falls, sunflowers turn toward one another for support. It turns out that may not be true. But I still love the idea, because it says something that *is* true about people.

There are days when we simply run out. We run out of hope, out of strength, out of reasons to keep going. On those days, we borrow what we don't have from someone else: a friend's belief, a stranger's kindness, a therapist's reassurance, a parent's hug, a book that understands us. We lean on one another until we can stand on our own again.

No one is meant to carry every burden alone. Sometimes the reason you survive today is because someone else is carrying the hope for you.

One day, the roles will reverse. The strength you borrowed will become the strength you offer. Just as someone once held a light for you, you will become a light for someone else.

Maybe that's why sunflowers inspire me. Not because of a story about how they behave in the dark, but because they remind me that even when I cannot find the sun, I can still find people.

And sometimes, people become sunlight.

Because, Mental Health Needs Unashamed Conversations

I want to live long enough to see the day when mental health is spoken about as naturally as physical health. When saying, "I'm struggling," is met with the same compassion as saying, "I'm unwell."

I want people to stop whispering the words *depression*, *anxiety*, *bipolar disorder*, *OCD*, or *burnout* as though they are something shameful. I want them to be believed without having to prove that their pain is real. I want people to understand that not every wound leaves a bruise.

I want us to stop asking, "What's wrong with you?" and start asking, "How can I help?"

I want a world where we don't disappear when someone is in a mental health crisis. Where we don't become uncomfortable and slowly drift away because we don't know what to say.

I want us to show up anyway.

I want us to bring flowers and chocolates to someone who has just come home from a psychiatric admission the same way we would after surgery. I want us to cook a meal, do their laundry, walk their dog, or simply sit beside them when getting out of bed feels impossible. I want practical acts of love to become ordinary, not exceptional.

I want medication to exist without shame. I want people to take antidepressants or mood stabilizers with the same ease that someone takes medication for high blood pressure or diabetes. No lectures, no judgment, no exhausting conversations where they have to defend why they need help.

Most of all, I want mental health to become part of everyday conversation. Not only during awareness campaigns or after tragedy, but around dinner tables, in classrooms, at workplaces, among friends, and within families.

Because healing should never have to happen in silence.

And maybe if enough of us keep talking, one honest conversation at a time, silence will stop being the loudest voice in the room.

Because, Everest Base Camp

I promised someone I'd hike to Everest Base Camp with them one day.

It's a promise that lives somewhere in the future.

One day, we'll wake up before sunrise, lace up our boots, and begin walking. We'll complain about the steep climbs, laugh at how out of breath we are, take far too many photographs, and keep telling each other, "Just one more step."

Maybe we'll drink hot tea in tiny mountain lodges. Maybe we'll stare at peaks that make us feel wonderfully small. Maybe we'll reach Everest Base Camp tired, emotional, and completely overwhelmed by the fact that we actually made it.

Or maybe the trek itself won't be the most important part. Maybe the real reason is that I promised someone *I'd still be here.*

There are dreams that keep us alive not because, they are extraordinary, but because someone is waiting to share them with us. This is one of mine.

So I have another reason to keep going. There's a mountain with my footprints still missing.

Because, She Never Hangs Up First

I don't think she knows she does it.

At the end of every phone call, there is always that familiar pause. We say 'see you soon' once. Then twice. Somehow, another conversation begins. Another question. Another laugh. Another few moments stolen before the call has to end.

And then comes the silence. The kind where neither of us is really saying anything anymore. She's still there.

Waiting for me to end the call. Every single time. Just like Disney characters never leave the hug first, they let the children pull away first.

It sounds so ordinary when I write it down. It's only a phone call. It's only a few extra seconds. But I've learned that love rarely announces itself through grand gestures. Sometimes, it looks like someone who isn't in a hurry to leave you. I don't know if she waits because she's being polite, because it's become our little habit, or because she wants to hold on for just a few seconds longer.

Maybe it doesn't matter. What matters is how it makes me feel. It makes me feel like my presence isn't something to be rushed through. Like spending time with me isn't a task she's eager to finish. Like I am worth lingering for.

There have been days in my life when I have felt like a burden. Days when I have apologized for taking up too much space, for talking too much, for needing too much.

And then there is this quiet, almost invisible act. She stays.

For hours. Not because she has to. Just long enough for me to know that leaving isn't the first thing on her mind. Maybe that's what love is, not always in the words we say. Sometimes, in the moments we delay saying 'see you soon'.

And perhaps that's all any of us are really looking for. Someone who stays… even for just a little longer.

Because, I Want to Be the First Double Doctor In My Bloodline

When I graduated with my MBBS, I remember thinking, *We actually did it.*

Every version of me that stayed, I made it.

But somewhere inside me, another dream still quietly exists. I want to earn a PhD. Because I'd like to be the first in my family to do it. The first person in my bloodline to become a doctor twice.

That thought makes me smile.

Sometimes I imagine the day I'll finally hold that degree in my hands. I think about everyone who believed in me. And maybe, one day, someone in my family will look at my journey and think, *If she could do it, maybe I can too.*

I'd like to leave behind more than a surname. I'd like to leave behind the possibility.

Because, My Younger Self Deserves Better

Sometimes I think about the little girl I used to be.

The one who painted without worrying whether it was good enough. The one who laughed until her stomach hurt. The one who believed the world was kind, that people were good, and that life would only keep getting more beautiful.

She had so many dreams. She couldn't wait to grow up.

If I could sit across from her today and tell her that, one day, I would wonder whether life was worth living… I think she'd be heartbroken.

Not because she'd judge me but because she'd want to hold me.

She'd probably look at me with those big, innocent eyes and say, *"But there's still so much we haven't done."*

Sometimes I forget that she's still a part of me. She didn't disappear. She just got buried beneath grief, heartbreak, illness, and years of trying to survive.

I'd like to find her again. I'd like to protect her hopes instead of burying them. I'd like to show her that we kept the promises she made to herself.

That we became a doctor. That we kept painting. That we fell in love with life again, even if it took us a long time. I owe her that.

Because she spent her childhood believing that life would be beautiful. I'd like to stay long enough to prove that she wasn't wrong.

Because, I Haven't Found My Voice Yet

For most of my life, I have been the kind of person who tried not to take up too much space. I learnt how to be agreeable, how to smile when I wanted to disagree, how to swallow my opinions before they ever reached my lips. I convinced myself that keeping everyone else comfortable was more important than being honest about what I felt.

It seemed easier that way. If I stayed quiet, there would be no arguments, no disappointment, no risk of being "too much." So I became smaller, little by little.

The strange thing about making yourself smaller is that, eventually, you start disappearing from your own life. You wake up one day and realise you've spent years being who everyone else needed you to be, but you have no idea who *you* are when no one is watching.

I'm tired of that. Because surviving quietly isn't the same as living truthfully. There are still so many things I want to say. There are conversations I've only ever had inside my own head. Questions I've been too afraid to ask because I didn't want to sound difficult. Opinions I've hidden because I worried they would make people uncomfortable.

But maybe some things *should* make us uncomfortable.

I want to write about the things people are scared to admit out loud: about loneliness, about grief, about burnout, about wanting to disappear, and then finding one small reason to stay.

I want someone to read my words one day and quietly think, *"I thought I was the only one."*

Because I know what that feeling is like. I know what it feels like to desperately search for proof that someone else has survived the same darkness you're standing in. To crave a sentence that makes you feel understood. To realise that being seen can sometimes keep a person alive.

If I can become that sentence for even one person… Then my voice will have mattered. I don't want to spend my whole life apologising for existing. I don't want to shrink every time I have an opinion. I don't want to edit myself into someone easier to love. I want to learn how to speak, even if my voice shakes. I want to say the difficult things.

Not the kind of rebel who shouts the loudest, but the kind who refuses to stay silent simply because silence is more convenient.

For years, fear has spoken on my behalf. Now, I'd like to give courage a turn. There is still a version of me I haven't met yet. A woman who speaks without apologising. Who writes without censoring herself.

Who believes her thoughts deserve to exist just as much as anyone else's.

I don't know exactly what she sounds like yet. But I know she's in there. Waiting. I think she deserves the chance to be heard and I deserve the chance to become her.

Because, I Love My Bed Way Too Much

It sounds almost ridiculous when I say it out loud, but one of the reasons I stay is because I love my bed. Just because it's the one place that has never expected anything from me. It has never asked me to be productive, cheerful, strong, or okay. It simply lets me exist.

My bed has known every version of me. It has held me on nights when I cried so hard my pillow was damp by morning. It has caught my silent tears when I didn't have the energy to explain them to anyone. It has been there through the nights I wished I wouldn't wake up, and through the mornings when, somehow, I did.

It has also witnessed my happiest moments. The excitement of opening exam results, the relief of finally getting good news, the laughter from late-night phone calls that went on for hours, the afternoons spent reading "just one more chapter" until the sun disappeared, the comfort of watching my favourite shows for the tenth time because familiarity felt safer than uncertainty.

Some of my best memories happened there. Some of my worst did too.

There were days when my bed wasn't just somewhere I slept. It became my refuge. The world outside felt too loud, too demanding, too overwhelming, and the only place that felt remotely safe was underneath my blanket. For a while, my entire world shrank to those few square feet. Looking back, I don't think I was lazy. I think I was trying to survive in the only way I knew how.

People often say, "Don't stay in bed all day," as if it is always a sign of giving up. But sometimes, staying in bed is what keeps you here long enough to try again tomorrow. Sometimes healing begins with allowing yourself to rest without guilt.

My bed has never judged me for the days I couldn't function. It has never made me feel guilty for needing a break. It has quietly held every version of me, even the ones I struggled to love myself.

It's where I've grieved, where I've healed, where I've dreamed about a future I wasn't always sure I'd live long enough to see. It's where I've learned that surviving doesn't always look brave, sometimes it looks like pulling the blanket over your shoulders, crying until you're exhausted, falling asleep, and waking up willing to try one more day.

I hope there are still countless mornings ahead where I wake up slowly, stretch beneath the covers, and realise that life, despite everything, is still worth showing up for.

Because my bed has carried me through some of the darkest nights of my life, I'd like to give it the chance to witness many more peaceful ones too.

Because, What If Tomorrow Is Better?

I don't know if tomorrow will be better. No one does.

There have been days when I've gone to bed convinced nothing would ever change, only to wake up to a message that made me smile, a conversation that made me feel understood, or a tiny moment that reminded me life isn't always as heavy as it feels.

The funny thing about tomorrow is that it never tells you what it's bringing.

I've learned that life can change. Not through grand miracles, but through ordinary moments that slowly make your heart feel lighter.

If I had given up yesterday, I would have missed every good thing that came after it. So when everything feels hopeless, I hold on to one small question.

What if tomorrow is the day things begin to get better?

I don't need certainty. Sometimes, a '*what if?*' is enough.

Because, I Have Concert Tickets For Next Year

It's funny how a concert ticket can become so much more than a concert ticket.

For years, seeing my favourite artist perform live sat quietly on my bucket list. It was one of those dreams I always imagined happening 'one day'. I never really thought about when. I just hoped that eventually, life would line up and I'd get to experience it.

Now, I have the tickets.

Sometimes I look at the confirmation email and smile. Not because of the seat number or the venue, but because it represents a future. It reminds me that somewhere along the way, I believed I'd still be here next year.

I catch myself imagining the night already… the lights dimming, the crowd erupting, the first song beginning, and that overwhelming feeling of *I'm actually here.* I want to sing every lyric until my voice gives out. I want to be surrounded by thousands of strangers who, for one night, all love the same music I do. I want to leave with aching feet, blurry videos I'll probably never watch again, and a heart that feels impossibly full.

Life has taught me not to take those moments for granted.

There was a time when planning for next week felt impossible, let alone next year. So having something to look forward to, something I've dreamed about for so long feels significant.

I want to be there.

Because, What If My Pain Doesn't End With Me?

There have been moments when I've wondered if leaving would finally bring me peace. But then another thought always follows.

What if my pain doesn't end with me?

What if it simply finds a new home?

I think about the people I love. The ones who would spend the rest of their lives wondering if there was something they missed. Something they could have said. Something they should have done differently.

I know they would replay our conversations over and over, searching for answers that don't exist. They would carry questions no one could ever answer.

I know it would be unbearable for them, because it was unbearable for me. I would never want that for them.

They didn't create my pain. They don't deserve to inherit it. I don't want my absence to become the heaviest thing they ever have to carry. Maybe I can't stop myself from hurting all the time. But I can stop my hurt from becoming someone else's lifelong heartbreak.

One day, I hope my loved ones remember me through laughter, shared meals, inside jokes, and stories that make them smile, not through unanswered questions, a statistic and unbearable grief.

Because, Healing Takes Time

It's messy. It's slow. It asks for more patience than I ever thought I had.

Some days it feels like you're making progress. Other days it feels like you've taken ten steps backwards. The hard part is remembering that a setback doesn't erase how far you've already come.

I've learned that healing isn't about becoming the person you were before the pain. It's about becoming someone who has learned to carry it a little more softly.

The truth is, flowers don't bloom overnight. Bones don't mend in a day. Seasons don't change because we're impatient. Why should brains be any different?

Maybe I'm frustrated because I'm still healing. But maybe the fact that I'm healing at all means there's something worth waiting for.

So I'll give myself time. I'll give myself grace. Because healing asks for patience. Because real healing pauses, paces and pampers your mind.

Because, I Want To Run A Marathon One Day

It probably sounds ridiculous.

Especially coming from someone whose body has spent more time recovering than running. A body that has known hospitals, medications, setbacks, and days when simply walking across the room felt like enough.

But somewhere in my heart lives this quiet dream. I want to run a marathon.

I know I probably won't be the fastest person there. I just want to know what it feels like to cross that finish line and think, *My body, my mind and I did this.*

For so long, my body has felt like something I had to fight. Something that let me down. Something that couldn't keep up with the life I wanted to live.

Maybe a marathon wouldn't erase any of that, but it would remind me that my body is more than the illnesses it carries.

Even if I cross the finish line long after everyone else, I'll still have finished.

Because, My Doctors Haven't Given Up on Me

Over the years, I've met more doctors than I can count. Some have known me only briefly. Others have walked beside me for years, watching my health rise and fall, celebrating the small victories and helping me through the setbacks.

They've seen me on my worst days. The days when I arrived exhausted, frightened, and wondering if things would ever get better.

Yet, every single time, they showed up. My GP, specialists, nurses and even the group D workers who remembered my name. The people who looked at me not as a diagnosis, but as a person with a life worth fighting for.

What moves me the most isn't just their knowledge. It's their hope.

Every appointment ends with the same quiet determination: *"Let's keep trying."* Every new treatment, every referral, every plan is built on the belief that my future is worth investing in.

Sometimes, when I've struggled to believe in my own recovery, they've believed for me. They held on to hope until I could hold it again.

I know medicine doesn't come with guarantees. Not every treatment works. Not every answer arrives when we want it to.

But it is profoundly comforting about knowing that a whole team of people want to see me get better. I want to give them the chance to see that day.

Maybe, one day, we'll all get to celebrate together.

Because, I Think My Houseplants Like Me

My mum keeps them alive. But I'm convinced they grow for me.

I celebrate them like proud little achievements. Sometimes I swear they stand a little taller after I've admired them.

Maybe that's completely made up.

But I'd rather live in a world where plants enjoy being loved.

Because, I Want To Read My Poems Out Loud

I've always admired people who can walk onto a stage, take a deep breath, and speak as though they belong there. I've never felt like one of them.

My heart races before I've even reached the microphone. My hands become cold. My voice trembles before I've said a single word. Stage fright has always convinced me that everyone is watching, waiting for me to make a mistake.

So I've kept my words to myself.

I've written poems in notebooks, typed them into my phone, poured pieces of my heart onto paper, only to let them live there, unseen and unheard.

But deep down, I've always had this quiet dream. I want to stand in front of a room full of strangers and read one of my poems aloud.

I want my voice to shake at first and then steady itself. I want to look up and see people listening, not because my words are flawless, but because they recognise something of themselves in them.

I don't want fear to have the final say over my life. I want to know what it feels like to choose courage, even while I'm terrified.

And after spending so much of my life hiding… I think I'd like to know what it feels like to be heard.

Because, I Want To Know What Safety Feels Like

Not the kind of calm where I'm simply pretending everything is okay. Not the kind where I smile while my body is still bracing for the next thing to go wrong.

I want to know the kind of safety that reaches my nervous system. The kind where my shoulders finally soften without me noticing, where my heart doesn't race at every unfamiliar sound, where I don't have to stay on guard all the time.

I want to know what it feels like when my body pauses before it reacts. When I can take one slow, steady breath before deciding whether something truly deserves my energy. When I don't instinctively snap, shout, or shut down because my system no longer believes it's fighting for survival.

I want to experience a life where peace isn't something I have to force, but something my body finally trusts. I want to know what it feels like to exist without constantly waiting for the next emergency.

I want to live long enough to meet that version of myself, the one whose body has finally learned that it is safe.

How beautiful would that be?

Because, I Don't Want My Illnesses To Define Who I Am

I am not my diagnoses. I am not a list of medical conditions, a hospital file, or a collection of symptoms waiting to be managed.

I am someone to whom difficult things have happened. I live with complex trauma and debilitating neurological conditions, and they have shaped parts of my life. But they do not get the final say on who I am.

They don't get to define my character. They don't get to erase my dreams, my values, or the person I choose to be every day.

I want to be known for my kindness before my conditions, for my compassion before my pain, for the way I make people feel seen, the way I love, the way I listen, the way I keep showing up even when my body makes it incredibly difficult.

If someone remembers me years from now, I hope it isn't because of the illnesses I carried. I hope it's because I was gentle when the world needed gentleness, because I cared deeply, because I left people feeling a little more understood than before they met me.

My diagnoses are part of my story, but they are not the title of it. They explain some of what I’ve endured, but they will never define who I am. That is something only I get to decide.

Because, I Want Someone To Gift Me A Sunflower

Not the kind that wilts after a few days and ends up pressed between the pages of a book. I want the crocheted one. The one stitched together patiently, loop by loop, with someone's time and thoughtfulness woven into every petal.

A flower that doesn't fade, one that I can keep on my bedside table or my bookshelf for years, quietly reminding me that I was loved enough for someone to choose something that would last.

I'd spray it with my favourite perfume every now and then, so on the difficult days I could pick it up, hold it close, and pretend it had its own gentle fragrance. A small comfort, something familiar to reach for when the world feels heavy.

Maybe to someone else it's just yarn shaped like a sunflower. But to me, it would be proof that love doesn't always have to be grand. Sometimes it looks like a handmade flower that never dies, carrying the scent of happier days and the quiet reassurance that there are still beautiful things worth holding on to.

I want to live long enough to receive that sunflower and every bit of love it represents.

Because, I Want More Silly Moments

I want more evenings that don't look important from the outside. More card games where everyone gets way too competitive. More arguments over rules that nobody actually remembers. More laughter that starts over something completely ridiculous.

I want more late-night conversations with my brother while we play catch-catch, pretending we are just passing time when we are actually creating memories.

I want more moments that don't make it into photographs. The ordinary ones. The ones we don't realise are special until we look back and miss them.

Maybe life isn't only made of big achievements and life-changing moments. Maybe it is also made of cards on the table, laughter in the background, and someone throwing a ball back to you at midnight.

And I want more of those. More time with the people who make life feel like home.

Because, I Want To Build A Home

A home filled with the little things that make a life, not just a house made of concrete and walls.

A place where every corner holds a memory. A bookshelf filled with books I've slowly collected over the years, plants by the window that I remember to water, a favourite mug that has seen countless mornings, soft blankets, familiar scents, photographs that tell stories, and laughter that lingers long after the moment has passed.

It doesn't have to be big. It could be a tiny apartment with just enough room for everything that matters. What would make it special isn't its size, it would be that it's mine. A place built from my own hard work, paid for with the money I earned, a quiet reminder of everything I survived to get there.

I want a home that feels like an exhale. Somewhere I don't have to brace myself. Somewhere I can leave my shoes by the door, make myself a glass of lemonade, and know that I belong there.

I want to fill it with ordinary, beautiful moments: watering plants, cooking meals, hosting the people I love, reading on rainy afternoons, and falling asleep knowing that I've built a life that feels safe.

I want to live long enough to unlock the door to that home for the very first time, step inside, and think, *I made it here.*

Because, I Want To Earn My First Pay From My First Job

I want to know what it feels like to see my name on that first payslip and realise that I earned it. That after years of studying, surviving, recovering, and wondering if I'd ever get here, I finally did.

I know it probably won't make me rich. But that first salary will represent something far more valuable than money. It will be proof that I kept going long enough to build a future for myself.

Maybe I'll treat the people I love to a meal. Maybe I'll buy myself something small that I've wanted for years. Or maybe I'll simply leave it in my bank account and smile every time I see it, knowing that it came from my own hard work.

I want to experience the quiet pride of financial independence, the feeling of contributing, of standing on my own feet, of knowing that despite everything life threw at me, I still found my way into the working world. I want to live long enough to receive that first salary notification, look at it for a moment, and think, *This is the beginning.*

Because, I Want To Be A Good Mentor Someday

Because I know what it feels like to need someone who chooses compassion over judgment.

I've had mentors who saw me at my lowest and mistook survival for self-sabotage. Who told me to redefine my definition of a crisis while I was actively in one. When you're drowning, you don't need someone standing at the shore telling you to swim better. You need someone willing to throw you a life jacket.

I don't want to be the kind of mentor who only celebrates achievements. I want to be there for the ordinary days, the difficult days, and the days when everything seems to be falling apart.

I want to check in when someone goes quiet instead of assuming they're lazy or uninterested. I want to take them out for coffee when they need a break more than another lecture. If they're sick, I want them to know they don't have to face it alone. If they're celebrating a milestone, I want to be the first to cheer them on, because joy deserves witnesses too.

I was a student mentor once, and I still don't know if I did enough. Maybe I got some things right, and maybe there was so much more I could have done. But instead of letting that uncertainty stop me, I want to let it make me better.

I want the people I mentor to leave feeling more confident than when they arrived. I want them to know they were seen, heard, and valued not just for what they achieved, but for who they were.

Years later, I hope they won't remember me because I was the smartest person in the room. I hope they remember that I was kind. That I believed in them when they struggled to believe in themselves. That I made them feel less alone.

I want to live long enough to become the mentor I once needed.

Because, I Want To Know Life Beyond Grief

Right now, grief feels like it takes up every room inside me. It sits beside me in silence, follows me into ordinary moments, and sometimes makes it hard to remember who I was before I started carrying it.

But I don't believe this is the only version of me that exists.

I want to meet the woman who still remembers her losses but isn't defined by them. The one who can think about what happened without feeling like she's drowning in it. The one who carries her grief with tenderness instead of letting it carry her.

I know grief may never disappear completely. Maybe it isn't meant to. Maybe love and loss always leave their fingerprints on us. But I hope there comes a day when those fingerprints no longer feel suffocating.

I want to know what it feels like to laugh without guilt, to make plans without fear, and to wake up with hope instead of heaviness. I want to discover the parts of myself that have been waiting patiently beneath all this sorrow.

I want to live long enough to meet the person I become when grief is no longer the loudest voice in my life. Not because I've forgotten what I've lost, but because I've finally learned that there is still room for joy alongside it.

Because, Your Presence Matters

More than you'll probably ever know.

You'll never fully know the impact you've had on the people around you. The smile you offered when someone was having the worst day of their life. The text you sent just to check in. The conversation you don't even remember having gave someone the strength to keep going.

The smallest acts of kindness often leave the deepest marks. A few minutes of your time, a word of encouragement, sitting beside someone in silence, holding a door, remembering their favourite snack, listening without trying to fix them, small acts but they may have meant the world to someone.

You may never know that something you did became someone's reason to believe that the world was still worth staying in.

Your presence creates ripples that travel farther than you can see. Long after you've forgotten a moment, someone else may still be carrying it with them.

The truth is, your life has touched other lives in ways you'll never be able to measure. You matter not because you have to achieve something extraordinary, but because simply being here allows you to love, comfort, encourage, and change people in quiet, ordinary ways.

You may never know whose life became a little lighter because you were in it. But that doesn't make your impact any less real. Your presence matters far more than you'll ever know.

Because, It Would Break Her Heart

There are some people whose lives become intertwined with ours so quietly that we forget how deeply our existence is woven into theirs.

She is one of those people.

If I were gone, there would be an empty space in her life that no one else could occupy. Not because she wouldn't keep living, she would, but because she would have to learn how to live around a loss that never truly leaves.

My absence would become something she carries everywhere.

There would be moments when she instinctively reaches for her phone to tell me something, only to remember there is no one on the other end anymore. There would be milestones she would want to celebrate with me, ordinary days she would want to complain about, jokes she would want to send. And every time, she would be met with the same unbearable silence.

She would have to grieve not only the person I was, but every future we imagined together, the conversations we never got to have, the places we never got to visit, the promises that would remain unfinished.

Losing your soul sister isn't unbearable, it's heartbreaking. She would carry me into birthdays, holidays, quiet Sunday afternoons, and random Tuesday evenings. She would wonder what I would have said. She would miss me in a thousand ordinary moments that no one else would ever notice.

I don't want her to spend a lifetime learning how to not miss me.

I want us to grow old enough to laugh about stories we've told a hundred times. I want us to complain about aching knees, celebrate each other's victories, and sit together years from now, grateful that we both stayed.

Because some bonds are too precious to be ended by grief.

And I cannot bear the thought of leaving her with silence.

Because, Unbelievable Good Luck Might Be On The Way

The beautiful thing about the future is that it never tells you what's coming.

One ordinary day, your entire life can change. An email you've been waiting for finally arrives. A doctor says the words you've been hoping to hear. A stranger becomes a lifelong friend. An opportunity appears that you never thought you'd have.

None of those moments send a warning. They simply arrive.

I want to be here for the days that surprise me. The days that remind me life isn't only made of heartbreak. The days that make me look back and think, *I'm so glad I stayed.*

Maybe the chapter I'm in now isn't the whole story. Maybe somewhere ahead, life is quietly preparing something beautiful that I cannot yet see.

I don't want to miss the moment when everything begins to change.

Because, Someone Held The Lift For Me Today

It lasted only a few seconds.

A stranger noticed me walking towards the lift, pressed the button, waited, and smiled as I stepped inside. They didn't know anything about me. They didn't know what kind of day I was having or what I was carrying. They were simply kind.

It reminded me that the world isn't made up only of cruelty. Sometimes, it's made up of people who hold doors open, smile at strangers, and make room for someone else without expecting anything in return.

Most acts of kindness are so small that they're easy to overlook. But on difficult days, they can feel enormous.

I want to keep living in a world where people still choose kindness in ordinary moments. Because sometimes, all it takes is someone holding the lift for you to remember that there is still goodness here.

Because, My Therapist Reminded Me That This Won't Last Forever

Today, my therapist told me that I'm feeling this way because my nervous system is overloaded. It has been carrying too much for too long. It feels overstimulated, exhausted, and unsafe.

She didn't dismiss my pain or tell me to just calm down. She explained that this is an episode of distress: a long one, a difficult one, but still an episode. And episodes, no matter how overwhelming they feel, do eventually pass.

For the first time in a while, I felt a small crack of hope. Not because everything suddenly got better, but because someone reminded me that my current state is not a life sentence. I will not feel this way forever.

She was kind to me today. She reminded me to eat, even if I don't feel like it. To take my medications on time, even if I'm struggling. She helped me sort through the chaos in my head and focus only on the most important priorities, one step at a time.

Sometimes healing doesn't arrive as a grand breakthrough. Sometimes it arrives as a gentle voice saying, "Let's make sure you've had your medications today."

Because, I Want To Be That Girl Who Dances Again

There was a version of me who didn't overthink every movement. Who heard a song she loved and let her body respond before her mind had a chance to interrupt. I miss her.

I don't know exactly when she disappeared. Maybe life became too heavy. Maybe grief settled into my bones. Maybe my body stopped feeling like a safe place to exist.

But I don't believe she's gone forever. I want to meet her again. The girl who dances in her room while no one is watching, who laughs halfway through because she forgets the steps, who doesn't care if she's graceful, who moves simply because she's alive.

I want to know what it feels like when joy reaches my body again instead of stopping at my thoughts.

Maybe one day a song will come on, and without thinking, I'll start dancing. And maybe that will be the moment I realize that healing didn't arrive all at once. It arrived one small step at a time.

Because, I Want The Years Of Living To Outnumber The Years Of Surviving

For a long time, life has been about getting through the day.

Counting medications, counting appointments, counting hours until bedtime, measuring success by whether I made it through another twenty-four hours.

That isn't living. That's surviving.

Survival is necessary, and I'm proud of the version of me who fought so hard to stay here. She deserves more credit than she'll ever give herself. She carried me through days I never thought I would make it past.

But I don't want survival to be the only story my life tells.

I want the years ahead to be remembered for more than what I endured. I want them to be filled with things that have nothing to do with illness or recovery. I want ordinary mornings, spontaneous plans, work I care about, people I love, and memories that aren't measured in hospital admissions or difficult seasons.

I want to reach a point where, when I look back, I realise that the years I truly lived have become greater than the years I merely survived.

Not because those years of survival didn't matter, they did. They brought me here. But because they were never meant to be my forever.

Because, Songs Still Sound Melodious

There are days when the world feels unbearably heavy. And yet, somehow, a song still finds its way through.

Sometimes it's a melody I've heard a hundred times before. Sometimes it's a lyric that seems to understand me better than I understand myself. Sometimes it's just a few minutes where my mind quietens, and all I have to do is listen.

Music doesn't ask me to explain myself. It doesn't ask me to be okay. It simply sits with me.

There have been days when a single song has made me cry, and days when another has reminded me that joy still exists somewhere inside me. The notes haven't changed, but somehow, they've carried me through.

As long as songs can still move me, there is still something in me capable of feeling wonder.

I want to keep discovering melodies I've never heard before. I want to keep finding lyrics that put words to experiences I couldn't explain. I want to know what songs will soundtrack the happiest days of my life.

Because as long as music can still make my brain pause for a moment…

…there is still something beautiful worth staying for.

Because, Illness Is Not A Reliable Narrator

Mental illness has a convincing voice.

It tells you that you'll always feel this way. It speaks with such certainty that, in the moment, it can sound like the truth.

But it isn't.

I've lived long enough to know that my mind has told me things that later turned out to be false. Illness can distort the way you see yourself, other people, and the future. It can make hope feel impossible to imagine, even when it still exists.

I want to remember that I don't have to believe everything my mind says when it is unwell. I want to stay long enough for the fog to lift again, for perspective to return, and for my own voice to become louder than the illness.

Because the darkest thoughts are often symptoms. And I refuse to let a temporary state of mind write the ending of my story.

Because, I Want To Know What It Feels Like To Laugh Without Faking It

I miss the kind of laughter that catches you by surprise, the kind that escapes before you've had a chance to think, the kind that leaves your cheeks aching and your stomach sore, the kind that makes you forget, even for a moment, everything that has been weighing you down.

Lately, laughter has sometimes felt like something I perform instead of something I experience. I smile because it's expected. I laugh because it's polite. But somewhere inside, I'm still carrying the heaviness.

I don't want that to be forever.

I want the day when laughter comes naturally again. When I don't have to convince myself to join in. When joy arrives so unexpectedly that I forget to hold it back.

I know that day won't erase everything I've been through. But it will remind me that pain doesn't get to own every part of me.

I want to live long enough to hear my own laughter and realise it isn't forced.

It's real. And so is the life I've fought to keep.

Because, Car Rides Feel Like Endless Possibilities

When I'm in a moving car, my thoughts seem to slow down.

Instead of spiralling, I find myself watching the road ahead. For a little while, my mind stops feeling trapped.

The open road reminds me that life is still unfolding. That there are places left to go, people left to meet, and moments I haven't lived yet.

Somehow, every car ride makes the future feel possible.

Because, I'm Yet To Make More Mistakes

I've spent so much of my life trying to get everything right. To say the right thing, make the right decision, choose the right path. But somewhere along the way, I forgot that mistakes are part of being alive.

I haven't made all my embarrassing mistakes yet. I haven't taken every wrong turn. I haven't sent every awkward text, burnt every recipe, missed every train, trusted the wrong person, or changed my mind about something I once believed with certainty.

Making mistakes means I'm still growing. It means there are still lessons left to learn, people left to meet, and experiences that will shape me into someone I can't yet imagine.

One day, I'll probably laugh at some of the mistakes I haven't made yet.

Because, One More Time

I've stopped asking myself, "Can I do this for the rest of my life?"

It's too big a question. Instead, I ask,

"Can I have one more glass of water?"

"Can I just move a bit to reach my meds and take them?"

"Can I write one more post-it for myself?"

"Can I make it to bedtime?"

Life became gentler when I stopped asking forever to fit inside today. Forever is overwhelming. This hour isn't.

So today… just one more task. Tomorrow, you can ask me again.

Because, Not Now

I've spent so much of my life trying to make sense of everything. As if, somehow, if I could just understand it all, it would stop hurting.

But some things don't ask to be understood. They ask to be lived through.

I've realised that I don't have to have all the answers today. I don't have to figure out the rest of my life before I go to bed tonight. I don't have to untangle every thought that's racing through my mind.

Some things can wait. Some questions will answer themselves with time. And some may never have an answer at all.

Maybe that's okay. Maybe peace isn't always found in understanding. Maybe sometimes it's found in saying, *"I don't know, and I don't need to know right now."*

I can let today be today. I can let life unfold in its own time. I don't have to carry the weight of figuring everything out.

Because, There Are Eight Billion Versions Of Normal

For a long time, I thought I was doing life wrong. I looked at other people and wondered why everything seemed to come so easily to them. Why I couldn't keep up. Why didn't my life look the way I thought it was supposed to?

I spent years chasing a version of normal that was never mine to begin with. But then I realised something.

There isn't just one way to be human. There are eight billion people in this world, each carrying a different story, a different body, a different mind, a different pace. What feels normal to one person may feel impossible to another.

My life doesn't have to look like someone else's to be meaningful. My healing doesn't have to happen on anyone else's timeline. My version of normal is allowed to be different.

Maybe that's what being human has always been, learning that there was never one definition of 'normal'.

There are billions.

Because, I Haven't Had My Rebel Era Yet

Somewhere inside me is a version of myself who is waiting to be unleashed. The one who chops her hair without overthinking. The one who dyes it red just because she can. The one who says what she believes without immediately wondering if everyone will approve. The one who takes up space without apologising for it.

For so long, I have worried about being accepted, being liked, being understood.

But maybe life is not just about fitting into the spaces people create for us. Maybe it is about creating our own.

I want to be a little rebellious. The kind who questions things, the kind who speaks up when something matters, the kind who chooses herself even when it feels uncomfortable.

Maybe one day I will look in the mirror with bright red hair and think, *"There she is. The person who stopped asking for permission to exist."*

Because, A Part Of Me Still Loves Me

I don't always feel it. There are days when my mind is unkind to me. There are days where I question my worth, my future, and whether I'm enough.

But then I notice the quiet things. I take my medications. I show up to therapy. I reach out to someone when the weight becomes too much. I rest when my body asks me to. I keep looking for reasons to stay.

I've realised that everything I do, in some way, is an attempt to protect myself.

Maybe that's what love looks like when you're struggling. Not grand declarations or unwavering confidence, but small acts of care. Choosing to stay. Choosing to try again tomorrow. Choosing, over and over, to keep myself alive.

So, maybe I don't always know how to love myself. But somewhere beneath the fear and the pain, there is still a part of me that does.

Because, Hot Chocolate

Tea wants me to be calm. Coffee wants me to be productive. Hot chocolate? Hot chocolate has no expectations of me whatsoever.

It simply says, *"Here. Have some chocolate first."*

And honestly, I trust its judgment. I've never had a cup of hot chocolate ask me about my five-year plan. It's never suggested I should be making better use of my time. It has never once told me to think positive.

It just exists... as warm, melted chocolate in a mug. Which, if you ask me, is a pretty solid life philosophy.

Could I have a hot chocolate instead of dealing with my problems? No.

Will I have one before dealing with them? Absolutely.

Because some crises can wait five minutes.

And if they can't... At least I'll be facing them with chocolate.

Because, There Is No Deadline

I don't know who decided that by twenty-five, I should have my life figured out. Or by thirty. Or sixteen. Or ninety-nine.

Somewhere along the way, I started believing I was behind; behind on healing, behind on my career, behind on life. But behind who?

Everyone is living a completely different life, carrying a different story, and walking a different path. Why would our timelines ever look the same?

Maybe I'm exactly where I need to be. Maybe this season isn't asking me to have all the answers. Maybe it's only asking me to keep going.

I'll figure some things out this year. Others, ten years from now. And some things, perhaps, I'll spend my whole life learning. I don't need to rush becoming the person I'm meant to be. There is no prize for arriving first.

Because, Dreams Do Come True

Not the kind of dreams that wake you up at 3 a.m. with your heart racing. Although, unfortunately, those do come true sometimes too.

I mean the other kind. The ones you imagine when no one is watching, the little hopes you carry around without telling anyone because they feel too fragile to say out loud.

The things you once thought, *"Maybe one day..."* And then, somehow, one day arrives. You find yourself standing in a moment you once only pictured in your head. And you realise that in the past, you were not silly for hoping. You were simply seeing a future you hadn't reached yet.

Not every dream happens exactly the way we imagined. Some arrive differently. Some take longer. Some become something even better than what we planned. But I think there is something beautiful about knowing that the things we quietly wished for can find their way to us.

So I want to keep dreaming. Because somewhere ahead, there are still things I have only imagined. And maybe, one day, I will wake up and realise... I am living one of them.

Because, My Shopping Cart Deserves Attention

I've spent weeks carefully curating it: removing things, adding them back, convincing myself I don't need them, convincing myself I absolutely do.

It would be a shame to let all that emotional investment go to waste.

Because, There Are Still Parcels With My Name On Them

There's something oddly exciting about waiting for a package.

The little notification that says, *"Out for delivery."* The doorbell rings. Tearing open the cardboard box as if it's a birthday present, even though I was the one who bought it.

It's never really been about what's inside, it's about having something to look forward to.

A tiny reminder that joy doesn't always arrive in life-changing moments. Sometimes it arrives in bubble wrap, wrapped in brown cardboard, with your name printed on the label.

And I think life is a bit like that too. Maybe there are still things with my name on them that haven't arrived yet.

Because, My Photo Gallery Needs Rearranging

Every once in a while, I scroll through old photos, looking for one picture, and end up staying much longer than I meant to.

I find faces I haven't seen in years. Sunsets I'd forgotten about. Random selfies, blurry photos, terrible angles, and moments that felt ordinary at the time but somehow became precious.

It's strange how a single photograph can remind you that you've already lived through so much.

Maybe one day, while rearranging my photo gallery, I'll stumble across a memory that makes me smile. And maybe it'll remind me that there are still thousands of photos I haven't taken yet.

Moments I haven't lived... People I haven't met… Memories that don't exist…

yet.

Because, A Really Good Hug

There are some things words can never do, a really good hug is one of them.

The kind where you don't have to explain yourself. The kind that says, *"I've got you,"* without saying anything at all. The kind that lets your shoulders soften, if only for a moment.

I don't think we ever outgrow the need to be held. Sometimes, a hug doesn't fix what's broken but it reminds you that you don't have to carry it alone.

Because, I Am Yet To Forgive Myself

I think I have forgiven a lot of things in my life. But there is one person I still struggle to forgive.

Myself.

For the mistakes I made when I was trying my best, for the moments I didn't know what to do, for the times I look back on and wish I had reacted differently, chosen differently, or been kinder to myself.

I forget that I was also someone who was hurting. I was learning. I was surviving. I was trying to navigate things I had never faced before. And maybe I deserve the same kindness I would give to someone else in my place.

I don't want to spend the rest of my life being angry at a version of me who was just trying to make it through the day. I want to meet the person who can look back at her past self with softness instead of shame.

The person who can finally say,

"You did what you could with what you knew. I'm proud of you for making it this far."

Because, Someone Owes Me Serious Money

I don't know who it is yet. I don't know how much they owe me. But considering the amount of emotional damage, inconvenience, and unnecessary drama I've experienced...

I think the bill is going to be impressive.

Maybe life owes me compensation. A refund for the difficult days, interest for the sleepless nights, a little bonus for every time I said, *"I'm fine,"* when I absolutely was not.

And honestly? I would like to collect.

Preferably in the form of unexpected happiness, good health, a peaceful mind, and maybe a lifetime supply of chocolate.

So until I receive my payment... I guess I have to stay.

Because someone, somewhere, owes me serious money.

Because, A Cat Chose Me

I went to a cat café one day, not expecting anything extraordinary.

I just wanted to sit among the cats for a while. To watch them do what cats do best: ignore people, judge everyone silently, and decide when they want affection.

I sat there quietly, surrounded by them. And then she came over. A six-year-old lady cat named Frannie.

She didn't know me. She didn't know my story. She didn't know the difficult years I had lived through or the battles I was still fighting.

She just walked up to me. Then she came back again. And again. Out of everyone in that room, she kept choosing me.

It sounds like such a small thing.

Cats don't pretend. They don't give affection because they feel obligated to. They choose where they feel safe. And somehow, this little cat decided that I was a safe place.

For a few minutes, I wasn't someone trying to be strong. I wasn't someone carrying a thousand thoughts. I was just a person sitting with a cat who wanted to be near me.

Maybe I needed that reminder, that I am still someone worth choosing even on the days I struggle to choose myself.

Maybe, some day she would find her home with a human too.

Because, I Don't Want To Miss Meeting My Child

It might sound strange to some people.

But somewhere in my future, I can picture a little person who doesn't exist yet. A child who might inherit my laugh, my stubbornness, my love for small things, or maybe absolutely none of it.

I want to know what it feels like to hold someone and realise that the world is a little bigger because they are in it.

I want to teach someone things I had to learn the hard way. I want to pack lunches, listen to endless stories, answer impossible questions, and pretend I know what I'm doing. I want to be the person who makes a child feel safe, loved, and accepted exactly as they are.

I don't know what kind of parent I would be. I don't know what life will look like then. But I like knowing that there is a future version of me who might be sitting across from a tiny human, thinking:

"I almost missed meeting you."

And I want to stay long enough to meet them.

Because, I Have Not Finished Confusing My Therapist

No, seriously. At this point, I think my therapist has earned a medal. She has sat through my endless thoughts, my unexpected plot twists, and the impressive talent I have for finding a new thing to overthink every single week.

Sometimes I walk into therapy with a problem. Sometimes I walk in with a solution. Sometimes I walk in with a solution to the problem, a new problem with the solution, and three questions about why I have a problem in the first place.

It's a very organised chaos. I like to think of it as keeping things interesting.

My therapist probably thinks she has figured me out, and then I arrive with a completely unexpected emotional side quest.

But honestly? I'm grateful she stays curious. She reminds me that I'm not a puzzle to be solved. I'm a person to be understood. And maybe one day I'll finally run out of ways to surprise her.

But today is not that day. Because I have not finished confusing my therapist yet.

Because, The Mind Needs A First Aid Kit

We all know what to do when we get a cut. Clean it, apply antiseptic, bandage it. But when our mind gets hurt, we are often left standing there wondering what to do.

So, I want to teach people to build a little box, not filled with medicines, but with reminders that they matter.

A note from someone who loves them.

A playlist that brings them back to themselves.

A comfort item.

A list of things that have helped before.

A number to call when the world feels too heavy.

A tiny collection of things that say:

"Wait, stay. You have survived difficult days before."

Maybe it is time we prepare for the days when our minds need a little extra care too. And maybe one day, someone will open their little box on a difficult night and find exactly what they needed: *A reminder that they too can survive.*

Because, The Ocean Always Comes Back

The first thing I noticed about the ocean is that it never stays the same. Some days, it is calm and gentle. Some days, it is loud and restless. Some days, storms take over and the waves become overwhelming.

But the ocean never decides that a storm means it is broken. It doesn't apologise for its rough days. It doesn't compare itself to calmer waters.

It simply waits, changes, and eventually finds its way back to peace.

Maybe there is something I can learn from that. Maybe having difficult days doesn't mean I have failed. Maybe feeling overwhelmed sometimes is okay.

The ocean has been through countless storms, yet people still travel across it to find beauty. Maybe I can be like that too. Maybe the hardest seasons of my life can exist alongside moments of happiness, laughter, and love.

I want to stay long enough to discover that the storms were not the end of my story.

Because the ocean taught me something important: even the biggest waves eventually return to the shore.

Because, Past Me Would Be Proud

The younger me who once wondered if she would make it through would be amazed to see me today.

I may not have everything figured out, but I achieved things she once dreamt of and survived things she never thought she could.

She wouldn't ask me to be perfect.

She would simply smile and say, *"You made it this far."*

Because, That Promised Trip Needs An Itinerary

There is a trip I haven't taken yet, one that I promised my best friend we'd take.

One day, we will pack our bags, complain about how much we overpacked, argue about where to eat, get lost somewhere we have never been, and laugh about things that make no sense to anyone else. It probably won't be a perfect trip.

We might be tired. We might take the wrong route. We might spend too much money on something unnecessary. But that's what will make it ours.

I want to keep that promise. I want the memories we haven't made yet.

Because somewhere in the future, there is a day where we are sitting together, looking around at a place we once only talked about.

And I want to be there when it happens.

Because, I Want To Be A Safe Space

I have spent enough time trying to make my emotions smaller so they fit into other people's comfort zones.
"Calm down."

"Think positive."

"Don't overthink."

Ah yes, the three magical spells that apparently fix a human brain. If only feelings came with a mute button. But they don't.

And maybe that's okay.

I want to stay because I want to see a world where people don't have to apologise for struggling. Where someone having a difficult day is met with kindness instead of instructions. Where we don't rush people out of their pain, but sit beside them until they find their way through.

I want to be a part of those conversations. I want to remind someone that their feelings are not a burden. That they don't have to pretend to be okay to deserve care.

Because one day, I want someone to feel safer because I chose to stay. And maybe that is a reason worth holding on to.

Because, I Haven't Heard All The Ridiculous Advice Yet

One thing I have learned about struggling with mental health is that the moment people find out you are having a difficult time, everyone suddenly unlocks a hidden qualification.

Are they a Psychologist? No. Therapist? No. Medical professional? Definitely not.

But somehow, after watching one motivational video and reading a suspiciously confident WhatsApp message, they are ready to diagnose your entire existence.

And honestly? The creativity deserves recognition.

"Have you tried just not being stressed?" All these years of therapy, research, and conversations, and we were one sentence away from solving it.

"Just stop overthinking." Thank you. I will now inform my brain that its favourite hobby is cancelled.

"Think positive." Let me quickly walk into my brain's settings, click 'delete difficult emotions', and restart myself.

"Don't cry. Be strong." I will tell my tears that they need better discipline.

"Just go outside. Touch grass." I love nature. But unfortunately, the grass did not come with a software update for my nervous system.

"Have you tried yoga?" Yes. I have stretched my body. My problems, unfortunately, are not emotionally flexible.

"Drink more water." Hydration is important. But sadly, my emotional baggage did not dissolve after eight glasses.

"Wake up at 5 a.m. The universe rewards early risers." The universe and I clearly have different communication styles. Some days, waking up at all deserves a trophy.

"Just don't think about it." I will simply put my thoughts in a cupboard, lock the door, and hope they don't discover the spare key.

"Everyone feels sad sometimes." And everyone gets headaches sometimes, but we still invented medicine.

"You have to choose happiness." Where is the happiness aisle? Is it next to the cereal? Do I need a membership card?

"Don't make your problems your identity." But I would like to point out that I did not wake up one day and decide: "Today, I will make my

struggles my entire personality." Life handed me a very complicated character arc. I am just trying to play the game.

"Just pray about it." I believe in the power of prayer. But I also think sometimes God expects us to use the resources available to us, including doctors, therapists, and maybe not ignoring our problems until they develop their own personality.

"Have you tried a vacation?" Unfortunately, my brain packed itself into the suitcase and came along.

"Just keep yourself busy." The classic strategy of outrunning your thoughts. Unfortunately, my thoughts are marathon runners. They have stamina.

"Stop being so sensitive." I would love to. Unfortunately, my nervous system did not come with a sensitivity settings menu.

"You are thinking too much." Thank you for noticing. I was worried my overthinking was going unnoticed.

But as ridiculous as some of these advices can be, it has taught me something. People are often trying to help. They just don't always know how. And maybe that is why I want to stay. Because I want to be part of creating a space where people don't respond to pain with shortcuts. Where we stop trying to fix people in five minutes. Where we stop handing out advices when what someone really needs is a little kindness.

I want to have more conversations. More laughs. More moments where someone says, *"I don't know how to fix this, but I can sit with you through it."*

And honestly? I also want to hear what other creative solutions humanity comes up with. Because somewhere out there, someone is probably preparing to tell me that my mental health can be fixed by drinking lemon water while standing barefoot under the moon.

And I cannot miss that. The comedy is too good.

So yes. I will stay. Because apparently, the world still has unlimited ridiculous advice to offer and I have not finished laughing at it yet.

Because, Sabar

Patience.

A word I have heard a thousand times, but somehow still struggle to practise. Because I want things now. I want the healing now. The answers now. The version of myself I have been waiting for... preferably delivered with express shipping.

But maybe life doesn't work like that. Maybe, I don't need the healing to happen overnight. Maybe it takes as long as it takes.

Maybe some of the best things are quietly being built while I am busy wondering why they haven't arrived yet. Maybe there are conversations, memories, opportunities, and little moments of happiness that are still making their way to me.

I don't know when they will come. And honestly, I don't need to. For once, I want to stop chasing the future and trust that it is also moving towards me.

So, *sabar*.

Because I believe there is something worth waiting for. Somewhere ahead is a day where I look around and think, *"Oh. This is what I was waiting for."*

Because, Mediclaims Won't Claim Themselves

Apparently, surviving a health crisis was only the first challenge. The second challenge? Convincing an insurance company that, yes, the hospital bill is real.

I have entered the final boss level of adulthood: the mediclaim process. Honestly, I have fought enough medical battles. I refuse to be defeated by a PDF upload button.

So I will stay. Because my claims are pending. My receipts need organising. And unfortunately for the insurance company… I have too much experience filling out paperwork to give up now.

Because, Bitter Moments Leave Lessons Behind

I wish every difficult moment came with an explanation. A little note saying:

"This will hurt, but here's why."

Unfortunately, life does not work that way. Sometimes things are painful before they are meaningful. Sometimes we only understand a chapter after we've already lived through it.

The bitter moments taught me things I never wanted to learn. They taught me who stayed. They taught me what mattered. They taught me how much strength I had, even when I felt like I had none.

I wouldn't choose those moments again. But I also wouldn't erase everything they taught me. Because even the hardest chapters leave something behind: a version of me that knows more than she did before.

Because, I'm Still Under Construction

The title sounds funny, I know.

Sometimes I get frustrated with myself because I haven't become the person I hoped I'd be by now. I still have days where I struggle. And then I remember...

Construction sites are messy.

They're loud, dust settles everywhere, nothing looks finished. If you walked past one halfway through, you probably wouldn't be able to imagine what it was going to become.

But no one looks at a building that's still being built and says it's a failure.

They simply say, *"It's not finished yet."*

Maybe that's true of people, too. Maybe I don't have to have everything figured out at twenty-five, or thirty, or any age at all. Maybe I'm allowed to keep changing.

I think I've spent too much of my life believing I had to arrive somewhere. Maybe there isn't a final destination. Maybe being human is simply being a work in progress.

Brick by brick. Lesson by lesson. Day by day.

So if today feels unfinished, perhaps that's because it is. And I want to stay long enough to see what I'm becoming.

Because, This Isn't My Whole Story

Sometimes, when life has been difficult for a long time, it's easy to believe that this is all there is. That the pain is the story. That the diagnoses, the grief, the hospital admissions, and the endless fight to survive are somehow all that will ever define me.

But they aren't. They're chapters. Important ones and deeply painful ones. Chapters that changed me in ways I never asked for. But they are still only chapters.

I refuse to believe that the hardest part of my life gets to become the entire book.

There are still so many pages I haven't lived yet.

I don't know who I'll become in five years. I don't know which city I'll call home, who I'll meet, what work I'll do, or what ordinary moments will one day become my favourite memories. I don't know which dreams will come true, or which new dreams I'll discover along the way.

And that's exactly why I want to stay. Because I am curious.

Curious about the woman I'm still becoming. Curious about the life that is quietly unfolding, even when I can't see it. Curious about the chapters that haven't been written yet.

Maybe one day I'll read these words again from a place I can't even imagine today. Maybe I'll smile at this version of myself with so much tenderness. Maybe I'll wish I could reach back through time, wrap my arms around her, and whisper, *"See? We made it. There was so much more waiting for us."*

I want to give myself the chance to meet her.

Because every story has a chapter where everything feels impossible. The reader doesn't know how it's going to work out. Neither does the person living it.

But the only way to find out…

…is to keep turning the page.

Because this isn't my whole story. It's only the chapter I'm in today.

Because, What If It All Works Out?

I spend so much of my time preparing for things to go wrong. I have become very good at protecting myself from disappointment.

But sometimes, I wonder… What if I am spending so much time preparing for a future that never arrives? What if things actually do work out? What if the dream I almost gave up on finds its way back to me?

What if there are days ahead where I laugh without forcing it, wake up excited, and what if the version of myself I am waiting to become is already on her way?

I don't know what the future holds. But for once, I want to leave some room for something good to happen. Maybe not everything has to be a battle. Maybe some things can be gentle.

So instead of only asking, *"What if it all goes wrong?"* I want to ask a different question:

"What if it all works out?"

P.S. If I am in a crisis and someone says, "What if it all works out?" I'd probably hit them on their head. But it's a good way to see it in the bigger picture, because, "What if it really does work out?"

Because, My Story Is Untold

Somewhere out there, there might be someone who hasn't found my book yet. Someone who will pick it up on a difficult day. Someone who will read a few pages, underline a sentence, fold a corner, or save a paragraph because it said something that they needed to hear.

I think about that person sometimes. The person who might feel less alone because I decided to put my pain into words. The person who might realise that their darkest days are not the end of their story.

I don't know who they are. I don't know when they will find these pages.

But maybe that's the beautiful thing about stories: they travel to people when they are ready for them.

I want to keep writing because there are still words I haven't shared, lessons I haven't learnt, and moments I haven't lived. Maybe my story will help someone else carry theirs.

And maybe, somewhere, a stranger will hold my book on a difficult day and think, *"I'm glad she stayed long enough to write this."*

Because, I Have More Vision Boards To Make

I love the idea of a vision board.

A little collection of hopes, dreams, and slightly unrealistic ideas stuck onto a piece of paper and somehow convincing my brain that they are possible.

And the funny thing is… some of them actually happened. Things I once cut out, wrote down, and hoped for became things I got to experience.

Past me was apparently onto something. So now I have more boards to make. More places to pin. More dreams to imagine. More ridiculous little pictures that make me think, *"Wait… what if this actually happens too?"*

Maybe not everything will happen exactly how I planned. Maybe life will surprise me with something even better. But I want to keep creating them because there are still dreams I haven't put on paper yet.

And I want to be around to see which ones come true.

Because, Meds Need Time To Work Their Magic

Apparently, my brain did not get the memo that healing has a timeline. I would love for my medication to work like a software update: *Installing... 99% complete. Please restart your brain.*

Unfortunately, it doesn't work that way. It takes time. Time for my body to adjust. Time for my brain to find its balance. Time for tiny changes to quietly add up.

I think I sometimes expect too much from myself. I expect to wake up one morning and feel completely different, as if my brain is going to announce: *"Congratulations. The update is complete."*

But healing is rarely that dramatic. Sometimes it is small. A slightly easier day, a little more patience, a moment where something that used to feel impossible feels manageable. And those moments count.

So I will give my meds the time they need to work their magic. I will give myself the patience I deserve.

Because, I Don't Need A Hundred Reasons To Stay

One silly and random reason is enough.

For a long time, I believed that if I was going to stay alive, I needed a reason that was bigger than my pain.

A grand purpose, a life-changing dream, something so meaningful that it could somehow make all the suffering worth it.

I kept searching for that one perfect reason but I never found it. What I found instead were small reasons.

Almost laughably small. None of those reasons could explain an entire lifetime. But they didn't have to.

They only had to help me survive one more day.

I think we put too much pressure on ourselves to find one extraordinary reason to stay, when perhaps life has always been built from ordinary ones.

Tiny moments. Tiny hopes. Tiny acts of love.

When you're standing at the foot of a mountain, you don't climb it in one leap. You take one step and then another. Staying alive can be like that too.

You don't have to commit to the rest of your life today. You only have to find one small reason that makes you curious enough to see tomorrow.

Maybe tomorrow you'll find another. And then another. Until, one day, you look back and realise that all those little reasons quietly carried you through the years.

You don't need a hundred reasons.

On the hardest days, one is enough. And if today your reason feels silly, insignificant, or too small to matter, let it be enough anyway.

Because sometimes, the smallest reasons end up saving our lives.

Because, every life is worth living.

Because, I Hope, One Day, You'll Believe Me And Stay;

I know what it's like to read words like these and think, *They're meant for everyone else, not me.* I know what it's like to have hope feel distant. To have your mind argue with every reason, every possibility, every tomorrow.

I've been there too. That's why I wrote this book.

Not because I have all the answers, or because I never struggle anymore. I wrote it because, on the days I couldn't find a reason to stay, I borrowed one. Sometimes it was as small as a song. Sometimes it was a crocheted sunflower I hoped someone would give me one day. Sometimes it was the dream of a tiny apartment that would finally feel like home. Sometimes it was simply believing that this feeling would not last forever.

The reasons didn't have to be extraordinary. They just had to be enough to get me through one more day.

If you've made it this far, perhaps you're searching for a reason too. You don't have to borrow mine forever. I hope you'll find your own. But, you can borrow mine for as long as you need.

I hope one morning you wake up and notice that the weight isn't quite as heavy. I hope one day you laugh without forcing it. I hope life surprises you in ways neither of us can imagine. I hope you meet a version of yourself that is so grateful you stayed.

And most of all... I hope one day, you'll believe me when I say that your story is not over, when I say that this feeling can change, when I say that there are moments waiting for you that you cannot yet see.

I hope one day, you'll believe me.

And stay.

Because, Divya is Kind (Bonus 101)

I have known Divya for five years, but it feels as though I have known her forever. If there is one thing everyone notices about her, it is her kindness. She is, perhaps, kinder than the world has ever asked her to be.

She has endured immense challenges and pain while penning this book. Yet, it is that very kindness that gives a person the strength to transform moments of grief into words of hope for others. Hope is not something that comes easily to her during a crisis, yet she has an extraordinary ability to turn even the darkest moments into something that offers light to someone else.

Kindness is far more than a soft tone or gentle gestures. Kindness is reflected in our actions, in the choices we make every day. But before we extend kindness to others, we must first learn to be kind to ourselves: something Divya herself continues to struggle with.

Being kind to yourself means choosing compassion over judgment. It means looking for a perspective of hope even in the middle of a crisis. It means remembering that every life, including your own, matters. Forgiveness, gratitude, compassion, gentleness, and allowing yourself to move at your own pace are not signs of weakness; they are acts of self-kindness that bring comfort and healing. So, above all, be kind to yourself.

When kindness is absent, the world begins to feel much crueler. Years without experiencing genuine kindness can change the way a person sees themselves. A child may grow up believing that love must be earned rather than freely given. Emotional neglect slowly erodes hope, deepens loneliness, and intensifies psychological pain. In the absence of kindness, people stop believing they are worthy of care, understanding, or even a brighter future.

Yet every meaningful change begins with kindness. It teaches us how to nurture, how to care, how to help others grow, and how to show quiet strength. It inspires healing, encourages forgiveness, reminds us to value people as much as achievements, and gives us the courage to dream again. Kindness is often the beginning of hope.

That is why she has always said, **"Above all, kindness."**

- Chaitanyaa Ashish Sachde

Acknowledgements

This book would not exist without the people who carried me when I could no longer carry myself.

To my loved ones, thank you for keeping me alive on the days I didn't know how to do it myself. Thank you for sitting with me through the darkness, for believing in a future I couldn't yet see, and for reminding me, over and over again, that my life was worth fighting for. Your love held me together when I was falling apart.

To my soul sister, there are no words that could fully capture what you've meant to me. You have walked beside me through some of the darkest chapters of my life, never asking me to be anything other than honest. Thank you for answering the difficult calls, for staying when it would have been easier to walk away, and for believing in me even when I couldn't believe in myself. Thank you for proofreading every page of this book with such care and for writing its prologue, the 101st reason and about our previous and upcoming books. This book carries your fingerprints too, because your love is woven into every chapter.

To my therapist, thank you for creating a space where I could grieve without being rushed to move on. Thank you for helping me make sense of emotions that often felt too overwhelming to hold alone. Thank you for your kindness, your patience, and for reminding me to care for myself in the smallest, most practical ways: to eat something, take my medication, rest when I can. This book was written alongside my healing process, and your presence made this book possible.

Finally, ***to every reader who picked up this book***: thank you for trusting me with your time and your heart. If you've ever felt alone in your pain, I hope these pages have reminded you that there is someone else who understands. More than anything, I hope this book has given you one more reason to stay.

And if no one has told you this today: ***I'm glad you're still here.***

— Dr. Divya Vachhani

About The Author

Dr. Divya Vachhani is a doctor, mental health advocate, researcher, and writer who believes that some of the most important conversations happen in the quiet moments when people finally feel safe enough to say, *"I'm not okay."*

Beyond the hospital and research settings, Divya has volunteered as a student mentor and led initiatives promoting mental health awareness, believing that compassion is just as important as clinical knowledge. She hopes to build a career that combines medicine, research, education, and advocacy in service of those whose struggles often go unseen.

This book is perhaps her most personal work. It was born from some of the darkest seasons of her life and written as a reminder, to herself first, and to anyone reading it, that hope can coexist with pain, and that healing is rarely linear.

When she isn't writing, you'll probably find her with a book in hand, caring for her people, or dreaming about a future filled with meaningful conversations, research, poetry, and a home of her own.

Above all, she hopes that anyone who opens these pages closes them feeling just a little less alone.

If you have anything you'd like to share, maybe a review, or some of your reasons, you may email to me:

theofficialpsychonautdivya@gmail.com

A Note From The Author

This book was written by me, from my own life, experiences, thoughts, and hopes.

At times, I used artificial intelligence as a writing companion to help me find the right words for feelings that were difficult to express. It helped me organise ideas, improve the flow of sentences, and articulate emotions that often felt bigger than language itself.

Every story, memory, and reason in these pages comes from my heart. AI did not live these experiences, I did. It simply helped me shape them into words when I struggled to do so alone.

If these pages have made you feel seen, understood, or a little less alone, then they have fulfilled their purpose.

Thank you for reading my story.

More From The Same Author

On The Days You Can't: Letters I Never Sent

On the Days You Can't: Letters I Never Sent was the first book we wrote together, published anonymously under the names **Maya Kashyap** and **Radhika Thakkar**.

The story behind the book is just as meaningful as the book itself.

It all began in a hospital ward.

I was staying with my grandfather while he was admitted with severe mitral valve regurgitation. Our days revolved around ward rounds, Cath Lab updates, ICU visits, and long hours of waiting. Amidst the uncertainty, my best friend, Divya, shared something she had always dreamed of doing: writing a book.

She didn't want to write it alone. She wanted to write it with me.

My immediate response was, *"I don't even read books. How am I supposed to write one?"*

She smiled and said, *"We'll figure it out along the way. Let's just begin."*

And so, we did.

Ideas were exchanged between hospital corridors and phone calls. We discussed chapters while waiting outside the Cath Lab, refined our thoughts between ICU visits, and slowly watched a collection of scattered emotions transform into a manuscript. While Divya wrote from her home, I wrote from hospital corridors. Writing became more than a project, it became an escape, a source of comfort, and something we unexpectedly fell in love with.

Neither of us imagined how quickly everything would come together. Perhaps we both needed a little instant gratification during such an emotionally overwhelming time. In less than five months, we had written, edited, and published our very first book.

I still remember the evening our dream became real. We were in the middle of a family dinner when my phone lit up with a video call from Divya. As I've mentioned before, a video call from Divya is probably the most unexpected thing you could ever receive. I answered immediately. She was beaming with excitement and almost bursting to tell me that our book had gone live, it was finally available online. For a few moments, everything else around me disappeared. All the hospital corridors, the late-night edits, the countless phone calls, and every ounce of uncertainty suddenly felt worth it. The joy we felt in that moment is something I don't think either of us will ever be able to put into words.

The title itself came from one of our everyday conversations.

At one point, I said to Divya, *"There are some days you just can't."*

Those simple words stayed with us.

They perfectly captured what we wanted the book to represent, the days when life feels too heavy, when emotions remain unspoken, and when words never reach the people they were intended for.

That conversation eventually became our title: *On the Days You Can't*.

The book is a collection of letters carrying emotions, confessions, apologies, gratitude, and truths that we could never bring ourselves to say directly to the people they belonged to. Instead of sending those letters, we anonymously shared them with the world.

Looking back now, *On the Days You Can't* was much more than our first publication. It was our first collaboration, our first creative leap of faith, and the beginning of a journey neither of us could have imagined.

Most importantly, it became the seed from which *The Purple Butterfly* would eventually grow.

Every first carries a special place in your heart, and this book always will. It reminds us that even in the middle of hospital corridors, uncertainty and fear, something beautiful can begin.

— Chaitanyaa Ashish Sachde

Upcoming Book: Exclusive Sneak Peak

The Purple Butterfly:

Battles, Bruises and Becoming

The purple butterfly is a book written by Dr. Divya Vachhani and co-authored by Chaitanyaa Ashish Sachde. This book revolves around the theme of chronic illnesses and mental health. This book is a collection of stories, which may remind you that behind every diagnosis is a human being, behind every invisible illness is a battle rarely witnessed, and behind every butterfly is a story of survival.

Why *The Purple Butterfly*?

Purple represents the bruises nobody can see, the invisible wounds that do not appear on scans, do not bleed, and are so often dismissed because they cannot be seen. They are the pain carried silently every single day inside a body that the world insists looks perfectly fine. Purple also represents the battles fought to break free from the cocoon of pain, medical gaslighting, uncertainty, and suffering.

The butterfly represents transformation. A butterfly does not simply grow wings. It first dissolves completely inside its cocoon before becoming something new. Healing is often the same. Before there is growth, there is loss. Before there is hope, there is darkness. Before there is acceptance, there are countless moments of questioning, fear, and heartbreak.

This book is for every person living with a chronic illness, every individual struggling with their mental health, every family member and caregiver searching for understanding, every healthcare professional willing to listen, every advocate striving for change, and everyone who believes that empathy begins with hearing another person's story.

As the co-author of this true story, I have shared in her pain while often feeling completely helpless. There is a unique heartbreak in watching someone you love suffer when all you want is to make it stop. Time and again, I wanted to help, and protect, but I could not. Even today, I continue searching for ways to support her through a journey that has no simple map.

I have written these pages with love, frustration, helplessness, and hope, the emotions of someone who has stood beside this journey every step of the way.

— Chaitanyaa Ashish Sachde

www.ingramcontent.com/pod-product-compliance
Lightning Source LLC
LaVergne TN
LVHW022217200926
848481LV00006B/2010